God in Your Family

God in Your Family

By Dr. John R. Rice

Sword of the Lord
Box 1099
Murfreesboro, Tennessee 37130

Fourth printing 1982
ISBN 0-87398-304-1

Printed and bound in the United States of America

TABLE OF CONTENTS

Chapter **Page**

1/Thank God for Good Mothers! 9

2/"And Ye Fathers. . ." 37

3/"Home, Sweet Home" 55

4/God Blesses Big Families 83

5/Beautiful Women in Public and Private 105

6/Start a Family Altar Today 133

7/ABORTION—The Murder of the Helpless Unborn 153

8/Don't Let Satan Get Your Children 187

Family Tributes to Dad 217

AUTHOR'S PREFACE

In God's great mercy, this humble author has had two blessings or rather two great collections of blessings—first, in my father's home, and then in the home Mrs. Rice has helped me make through the years.

In 1945 my big book of 22 chapters, *The Home: Courtship, Marriage and Children*, was published and it has been, we believe, the most widely read and most influential book on the home through these twenty-six years.

But there is so much truth in the Bible, there are so many problems, so many blessings, and such vast importance in the question of a Christian home, that no book, no dozen books, can say all that ought to be said.

Here, then, are other chapters, a continuation, a sequel, to the first book, of other important chapters on *God in Your Family*.

Because the testimonies of Mrs. Rice and my daughters add some weight to my counsel in this book, I am printing them here. "Love wears colored glasses," it is true; but since our home has been greatly blessed of God, I want you to know that God's plan works.

My daughters are all married not only to Christian men but to full-time Christian workers. Two of them are teaching in Christian colleges; the other four are pastors. All six of my daughters hold the same moral standards that Mrs. Rice and I hold, the same devotion to the Bible. All of them are active soul winners.

God has given us twenty-seven grandchildren, and I am claiming God's sweet promise of "his righteousness unto children's children."

May the dear Lord put His blessings upon them to thousands of hearts and homes.

September, 1971 JOHN R. RICE

1/ *Thank God for Good Mothers!*

"I thank God. . .When I call to remembrance the unfeigned faith that is in thee, which dwelt first in thy grandmother Lois, and thy mother Eunice; and I am persuaded that in thee also."—II Tim. 1:3, 5.

Paul could thank God for Timothy's faith and his wonderful life and ministry, and so he could thank God for the grandmother Lois and the mother Eunice, who had taught Timothy to know and love the Saviour. Oh, we ought to thank God for good mothers!

Of the Ten Commandments, four of them have to do with our relation to God, and the last six, with our relationship to mankind. But the first of these six is, "Honour thy father and thy mother: that thy days may be long upon the land which the Lord thy God giveth thee" (Exod. 20:12). And we are reminded in Ephesians 6:2 that this "is the first commandment with promise."

The wife shares with her husband that marvelous privilege of bringing an immortal soul into being, in conception. The husband and wife are "heirs together of the grace of life" (I Pet. 3:7). Is it at the moment of conception, as we think, or at the time of quickening, or at the actual birth, that the child becomes an immortal soul? I think at the moment of conception. At any rate, God allows a woman, in her body, to partake of the creation of an immortal soul!

Motherhood, then, is greatly exalted in the Bible. It is the mother, as well as the father, who is to be honored, respected, obeyed, supported in her old age, by the children!

The Mosaic Law required the death penalty for murder. Exodus 21:12 says, "He that smiteth a man, so that he die, shall be surely put to death." And that teaching is repeated in Romans, chapter 13. But in the Mosaic Law, for a man to even smite his father or his mother, or to curse his father and mother, he was to be put to death. Exodus 21:15 and 17 says, "And he that smiteth his father, or his mother, shall be surely put to death. . . . And he that curseth his father, or his mother, shall surely be put to death." A godly reverence is required of children for their parents, and the mother in this, at least, is equal to the father.

And this authority of father and mother alike over a son even old enough to be a drunkard was such that in Deuteronomy 21:18-21 it was plainly commanded, "If a man have a stubborn and rebellious son, which will not obey the voice of his father, or the voice of his mother, and that, when they have chastened him, will not hearken unto them," then, they two should take that rebellious son before the elders of the city and have him stoned to death. Oh, God requires a godly reverence for parents and that reverence is for the mother as well as the father.

The Bible makes it quite clear that the ultimate authority in the home is the husband and father, but perhaps He made mothers more tender, more forgiving, just as they are more subjective and biased, and more tempted to be moved by affection and less by conscience and justice. So, ordinarily a father must set the principles on which the home is run and be the final authority. But, oh, the tender administration, the warmth and sweetness and fragrance and enduring godly influence of a good mother!

MY MOTHER

Who fed me from her gentle breast
And hushed me in her arms to rest,
And on my cheek sweet kisses prest?
My mother.

When sleep forsook my open eye,
Who was it sang sweet lullaby,
And rocked me that I should not cry?
My mother.

Who sat and watched my infant head,
When sleeping on my cradle bed,
And tears of sweet affection shed?
My mother.

When pain and sickness made me cry,
Who gazed upon my heavy eye,
And wept for fear that I should die?
My mother.

Who dressed my doll in clothes so gay,
And taught me pretty how to play,
And minded all I had to say?
My mother.

Who ran to help me when I fell,
And would some pretty story tell,
Or kiss the place to make it well?
My mother.

Who taught my infant lips to pray,
To love God's holy Word and day,

And walk in wisdom's pleasant way?
My mother.

And can I ever cease to be
Affectionate and kind to thee
Who wast so very kind to me—
My mother.

Oh no, the thought I cannot bear;
And if God please my life to spare,
I hope I shall reward thy care,
My mother.

When thou art feeble, old and gray,
My healthy arm shall be thy stay,
And I will soothe thy pains away,
My mother.

And when I see thee hang thy head,
'Twill be my turn to watch thy bed,
And tears of sweet affection shed—
My mother.

For God who lives above the skies,
Would look with vengeance in His eyes
If I should ever dare despise
My mother.

Jane Taylor

I. CONSIDER GREAT MOTHERS IN THE BIBLE

A godly woman will do well indeed to get her ideals and standards of Christian life and wifehood and motherhood from the Bible.

1. Jochebed, the Mother of Moses, Saved Her Son to Be God's Prophet

Some of us took a boat up the Nile River to the place

among the bulrushes where tradition says, some 3,600 years ago, a faithful mother planned and schemed and prayed and saved her baby boy.

We learn from Exodus 6:20 and Numbers 26:59 that her name was Jochebed, but the story in Exodus 2:1-10 leaves it so there she is known simply as the mother of Moses.

"And there went a man of the house of Levi, and took to wife a daughter of Levi. And the woman conceived, and bare a son: and when she saw him that he was a goodly child, she hid him three months. And when she could not longer hide him, she took for him an ark of bulrushes, and daubed it with slime and with pitch, and put the child therein; and she laid it in the flags by the river's brink. And his sister stood afar off, to wit what would be done to him. And the daughter of Pharaoh came down to wash herself at the river; and her maidens walked along by the river's side; and when she saw the ark among the flags, she sent her maid to fetch it. And when she had opened it, she saw the child: and, behold, the babe wept. And she had compassion on him, and said, This is one of the Hebrews' children. Then said his sister to Pharaoh's daughter, Shall I go and call to thee a nurse of the Hebrew women, that she may nurse the child for thee? And Pharaoh's daughter said to her, Go. And the maid went and called the child's mother. And Pharaoh's daughter said unto her, Take this child away, and nurse it for me, and I will give thee thy wages. And the woman took the child, and nursed it. And the child grew, and she brought him unto Pharaoh's daughter, and he became her son. And she called his name Moses: and she said, Because I drew him out of the water."

Is it not strange that nothing is said about the father's

part in saving the child? Jochebed looked at the little baby boy and "she saw him that he was a godly child." Did that mother have some sweet premonition from God that he would be blessed as a mighty law-giver and deliverer of the nation Israel? It seems that before the twins, Jacob and Esau, were born, Jacob's mother, Rebekah, inquired of the Lord and knew that the elder should serve the younger, that Jacob would prevail and be the head of a great nation. We do not condone her scheming, but she evidently knew better than did the complacent Isaac, that the blessing and the birthright should go to Jacob! (Gen. 25:21-23 and Gen. 27:1-33).

So Moses' mother must have had some sweet inkling of what God had in mind for the baby Moses, and she set out to work with God to spare him from the murderous Pharaoh who commanded all the boy babies to be killed! I cannot doubt that the sweet Spirit of God guided her as she made that little basket or ark of bulrushes waterproof and put the baby in it, and that as she set the little sister Miriam to watch, she made her plans ahead of time to take the baby back to her arms as nurse, and to train him for God, although he would now be called the son of Pharaoh's daughter!

Did my mother, who gave me to God when I was born and who called me her "preacher boy" many, many times before she went to Heaven when I was five, have some heavenly intimation that the hand of God would be upon me to preach His Word? I think so.

Oh, Mother, Mother, be sure you listen to the voice of God and cooperate with Him in rearing the little ones He gives you.

2. Hannah, the Mother of the Prophet Samuel, Gave Him to God to Be a Nazarite Before He Was Born!

Hannah was one of two wives of Elkanah, but she had no children. She wept much and would not eat. They went to Shiloh, the place of worship, and we read,

"And she was in bitterness of soul, and prayed unto the Lord, and wept sore. And she vowed a vow, and said, O Lord of hosts, if thou wilt indeed look on the affliction of thine handmaid, and remember me, and not forget thine handmaid, but wilt give unto thine handmaid a man child, then I will give him unto the Lord all the days of his life, and there shall no razor come upon his head."—I Sam. 1:10, 11.

The aged priest Eli saw her mouth moving but did not know that she prayed; he thought she was drunken.

And then at once she "went her way, and did eat, and her countenance was no more sad" (I Sam. 1:18). Oh, God had told her!

And so she conceived and a child was born and she named him Samuel which means "asked of God." And when he was weaned, perhaps after two or three years, she took him to Eli, at the place of worship, and said, "For this child I prayed; and the Lord hath given me my petition which I asked of him: Therefore also I have lent him to the Lord; as long as he liveth he shall be lent to the Lord. . . ." And each year she would bring him up a garment and rejoice that God would use the child of her prayers.

And Samuel is one of the few men, prominent in the Old Testament, about whom there was never a question, never a fault, never a mistake mentioned. Along with Joseph and

Daniel, he was counted blameless, the product of a mother's prayer and influence, no doubt. It is wonderful that the young man Samuel was soon converted and that he took for himself the vow that his mother had made for him: he would be a Nazarite to the day of his death, set apart for God.

3. Elisabeth, Too, Prayed and God Gave Her the Mighty Son, John the Baptist

John the Baptist was born in answer to prayer. Zacharias and Elisabeth were both "well stricken in years" and Elisabeth too old to have a child by any normal standards. But in answer to prayer, God gave the child. The story is told in Luke 1:5-17:

"There was in the days of Herod, the king of Judaea, a certain priest named Zacharias, of the course of Abia: and his wife was of the daughters of Aaron, and her name was Elisabeth. And they were both righteous before God, walking in all the commandments and ordinances of the Lord blameless. And they had no child, because that Elisabeth was barren, and they both were now well stricken in years. And it came to pass, that while he executed the priest's office before God in the order of his course, According to the custom of the priest's office, his lot was to burn incense when he went into the temple of the Lord. And the whole multitude of the people were praying without at the time of incense. And there appeared unto him an angel of the Lord standing on the right side of the altar of incense. And when Zacharias saw him, he was troubled, and fear fell upon him. But the angel said unto him, Fear not, Zacharias: for thy prayer is heard; and thy wife Elisabeth shall bear thee a son, and thou shalt call his

name John. And thou shalt have joy and gladness; and many shall rejoice at his birth. For he shall be great in the sight of the Lord, and shall drink neither wine nor strong drink; and he shall be filled with the Holy Ghost, even from his mother's womb. And many of the children of Israel shall he turn to the Lord their God. And he shall go before him in the spirit and power of Elias, to turn the hearts of the fathers to the children, and the disobedient to the wisdom of the just; to make ready a people prepared for the Lord."

The birth of John the Baptist was a time of great joy, and Zacharias, filled with the Spirit, prophesied wonderful things about John and particularly about the Saviour, whom John would announce.

But Zacharias had little faith and because he had not believed, was dumb for months before the child was born. We may well suppose, then, that Elisabeth had been even more fervent in prayer and had more faith. Very likely, she, too, had prayed for the kind of son she should have—one who would be "great in the sight of the Lord," who should "drink neither wine nor strong drink," who would be "filled with the Holy Ghost" and turn many of Israel to Christ! So, Spirit-filled Elisabeth "spake out with a loud voice" to praise God for the virgin Mary and the Saviour who should be born.

John the Baptist was a rather strange man. He lived in the desert until the time of his showing to Israel. He was dressed in a garment of camel's hair, with a leather girdle about his loins. His meat was locusts and wild honey. He was not, we suppose, the polished gentleman of the city but he was God's mighty prophet, given in answer to prayer and filled with the Spirit, like Elijah. Oh, who could tell what part Elisabeth's prayers and influence had on this mighty man of God!

II. WHAT A WONDERFUL HERITAGE OF RESPECT AND GODLY INFLUENCE HAVE AMERICAN MOTHERS HAD IN THE PAST

The Anglo-Saxon race, an English-speaking people, has had a wonderful regard for womanhood, and so for mothers. That is true largely because the Bible has had a more profound effect on Protestant Anglo-Saxon people than on any other culture in the world. That is reflected in our poems. How many heartfelt gems of literature have exalted motherhood and her godly influence.

Elizabeth Akers Allen wrote:

Backward, turn backward, O Time,
in your flight,
Make me a child again just for tonight!
Mother, come back from the echoless shore,
Take me again to your heart as of yore;
Kiss from my forehead the furrows of care,
Smooth the few silver threads out of my hair.
Over my slumbers your loving watch keep;
Rock me to sleep, Mother,—rock me to sleep.

Oh, yes, that was the day when mothers rocked cradles and didn't leave the baby in the nursery while she worked in the factory, or didn't hire babysitters while she went to the movies or her club. Then mothers nursed their babies at the breast and loved them, and mother's arms were the safest haven, the surest comfort that most people ever knew, except as they learned to trust the Saviour.

And again one writes:

If I were hanged on the highest hill,
Mother o' mine, O mother o' mine!
I know whose love would follow me still,
Mother o' mine, O mother o' mine!

The enormous influence of mothers is expressed in the songs of the years past, in the quotations by famous statesmen, in the eulogies of famous orators. Abraham Lincoln said, "All that I am or hope to be I owe to my angel mother."

Following the Civil War a very popular song tells:

The shot and shell were falling
Upon the battlefield.

But in the great battle the flag was shot down and the captain cried out, "Who'll save our flag?"

And the poem continues:

I will, a young man shouted, I'll bring it back, or die
And dashed into the thickest of the fray.
He saved the flag but gave his young life
All for his country's sake.
They brought him back and heard him softly say,
Just break the news to Mother
She knows how much I love her
Tell her not to wait for me
For I'm not coming home.
Just say there is no other
Can take the place of Mother.
Then kiss her dear, sweet lips for me
For I'm not coming home.

The gospel songs of the past day tell the same story—the enormous Christian influence of a godly mother. Was a boy wayward, a prodigal? Then this sweet appeal went out in many an evangelistic meeting:

Where is my wandering boy tonight—
The boy of my tenderest care,
The boy that was once my joy and light,
The child of my love and prayer?

Once he was pure as morning dew,
As he knelt at his mother's knee;
No face was so bright, no heart more true,
And none was so sweet as he.

O could I see you now, my boy,
As fair as in olden time,
When prattle and smile made home a joy,
And life was a merry chime!

Go for my wandering boy tonight;
Go search for him where you will;
But bring him to me with all his blight,
And tell him I love him still.

O where is my boy tonight?
O where is my boy tonight?
My heart o'erflows,
For I love him he knows;
O where is my boy tonight?

The mother of President McKinley lay dying. While he hurried about the great events of state and the duties of his country, he anxiously waited for the news about his mother. An engine and a private car waited at the railroad station, steamed up, and ready to go. A carriage waited at the door. A telegram came saying his mother was low and calling for him. He wired back, "Tell Mother I'll be there!" And the train rushed him to the Ohio town and by his mother's side for the last good-by.

The words of that filial president moved the heart of Charles M. Fillmore and he wrote this famous gospel song, "Tell Mother I'll Be There."

When I was but a little child how well I recollect
How I would grieve my mother with my folly and neglect;
And now that she has gone to Heav'n I miss her tender care:
O Saviour, tell my mother, I'll be there!

Though I was often wayward, she was always kind and good;
So patient, gentle, loving, when I acted rough and rude;
My childhood griefs and trials she would gladly with me share:
O Saviour, tell my mother, I'll be there!

When I became a prodigal, and left the old rooftree,
She almost broke her loving heart in mourning after me;
And day and night she prayed to God to keep me in His care:
O Saviour, tell my mother, I'll be there!

One day a message came to me, it bade me quickly come
If I would see my mother ere the Saviour took her home;
I promised her, before she died, for Heaven to prepare:
O Saviour, tell my mother, I'll be there!
Tell mother I'll be there in answer to her prayer—
This message, blessed Saviour, to her bear!
Tell mother I'll be there, Heav'n's joys with her to share,
Yes, tell my darling mother I'll be there.

Oh, godly mothers would do well to make sure that a saintly influence would hold their children so that they could not get away from Christ and Mother's God!

Charlie Tillman, anointed gospel singer, wrote another famous song that has moved the heart of thousands toward God.

MY MOTHER'S BIBLE

There's a dear and precious book,
Tho' it's worn and faded now,
Which recalls those happy days of long ago;
When I stood at mother's knee,
With her hand upon my brow,
And I heard her voice in gentle tones and low.

As she read the stories o'er,
Of those mighty men of old,
Of Joseph and of Daniel and their trials;
Of little David bold,
Who became a king at last;
Of Satan with his many wicked wiles.

Then she read of Jesus' love,
As He blest the children dear,
How He suffered, bled and died upon the tree;
Of His heavy load of care,
Then she dried my flowing tears
With her kisses as she said it was for me.

Well those days are past and gone,
But their mem'ry lingers still,
And the dear old Book each day has been my guide;
And I seek to do His will,
As my mother taught me then,
And ever in my heart His words abide.

Blessed book, precious book,

On thy dear old tear-stained leaves I love to look;
Thou art sweeter day by day,
As I walk the narrow way
That leads at last to that bright home above.

The famous Methodist evangelist, George R. Stuart, associate of Sam Jones, preached a message on the Christian home to five thousand people in the entertainment hall, Exposition Building, St. Louis, March 8, 1895, in the Jones-Stuart meetings. About the importance of the home, he said the following:

> I shall go with you tonight to the dearest and most sacred spot on earth to you and me—a spot around which cluster the sweetest associations and the most precious memories. I shall speak tonight of home. The longer I live, the more I visit from home to home, the more I see of the sorrows and cares, the successes and failures of this life, the more I am impressed that the home problem is the greatest problem of our civilization. The homes of our country are so many streams pouring themselves into the great current of moral, social, and political life. If the home life is pure, all is pure. The home is the center of everything.
>
> From the proper or improper settlement of the home question comes more of joy or sorrow, more of weal or woe than from all other questions combined. Build your palaces, amass your great fortunes, pile up your luxuries all about you, provide for the satisfaction of every desire: but as you sit amid these luxuries and wait for the staggering steps of a drunken son, or contemplate the downward steps of a wayward daughter, happiness flies out of your heart and your home. There is nothing that can render happy the parents of godless, wayward children.
>
> Around the home circle of the cottage or the palace are greater possibilities of joy or sorrow than in all the rest of the world. Not only does the happiness of the world center in the home, but the moral, social, and civil life of the world

emanates from the home. Every drunkard, every gambler, every debauchee, every lost character once sat in Mother's lap and learned the mother tongue and mother thought and mother action—the mother life. The downfall of every character can be traced to some defect in the home life.

If God Almighty has fixed it up so that we cannot take our children to Heaven with us, He has put us in a horrible condition. The prettiest picture earth furnishes is a whole family on the way to Heaven; the most horrible picture is a whole family on the way to Hell. I believe in the truth of the proverb of this Book: "Train up a child in the way he should go: and when he is old, he will not depart from it." A child properly trained up to the proper point will not go astray.

The normal way to get rid of drunkards is to quit raising them; the normal way to get rid of liars, thieves, and debauchees is to quit raising them.

And George Stuart and other great preachers knew then, as we know now, that a godly mother is one of the most important factors in a godly home.

I quote a wonderful testimony from Dr. Stuart in that meeting:

OH, IF I'D HAD A MOTHER

A poor young man stood before the judge to be sentenced to death; and when the judge asked if he had anything to say why the sentence of death should not be passed upon him, he bowed his head and said: "Oh, if I'd had a mother!"

Many a boy who has gone into a life of reckless folly, without restraints of home, can stand up in his debauch tonight and say, "Oh, if I'd had a mother! Oh, if I'd had a mother!" Some boys can say as the tramp said, when asked how long he had been an orphan, "I was born an orphan." I am profoundly thankful above all things for the fact that I have a good mother—a mother who, when she said, "George, you shall not," saw that I did not. If I did, then she did. I owe all that I am morally and religiously, to the authority of a good mother.

I also owe my life to that authority. I give this little history, which is sacred to me. A few years ago three other young men and I planned a trip to Europe. We had read and talked and planned for months. A few months before we were ready to start, I mentioned the trip to my mother, who since my father's death has made her home with me—and it has been my sweetest pleasure to give her the sunniest and best room in my home. When I mentioned the trip, she said: "George, I am getting old; you are my only stay: I am afraid of the ocean; I cannot let you go while I live. Wait till I am gone, and then you can go to Europe."

I thought it was a mere kind of sentiment with Mother, and decided that I would get all things ready for the trip, believing that in the kindness of her heart she would yield her consent. I had made arrangements, temporarily, as some of you possibly have done permanently, to have my father-in-law take care of my wife and children, and all things were ready for the trip.

A short while before we were ready to start I stated in the presence of my mother: "Well, we are off soon for Europe."

She looked up and said: "What is that, George?"

I said: "We have everything ready; the trip is all organized, and we start for Europe soon."

Straightening up in her chair, she looked me straight in the face and said: "George, I told you once I did not want you to go. I have thought over this trip and prayed over it, and I cannot give my consent for you to go; and now I tell you so that you will understand it: You shall not go."

I said: "Mother, do not put it that way." I tried to argue the question, saying: "It is one of the sweetest hopes of my life that you are crushing."

She said: "George, I have prayed over it; my mind is made up. We will not discuss it; you shall not go, and that settles it."

And when she said that, I knew it did settle it, and

surrendered what to me was one of the most pleasant hopes of my life. I hunted up my companions and said: "I'm not in it."

They excitedly exclaimed: "What's the matter?"

I said: "Mother won't let me go."

They said: "Are you not twenty-one, married and got children and yet tied to your mother's apron strings?"

I said: "I would not cross the old Atlantic against my mother's wishes for a million dollars."

A few days later I got a letter from Brother Jones, asking me to accompany him on a trip to Canada. The following week we were plowing across Lake Ontario. It was a bright day. Brother Jones, wife, and I were sitting on the deck of the vessel, and as she plowed through the blue waters I said, "This is glorious; how I wish it were on the Atlantic, and I were headed for Europe. I shall always feel that Mother was a little harsh in breaking up my European trip."

Brother Jones said: "Well, old boy, the whales might have gotten you in the Atlantic." On our return we were going in to the supper table at Buffalo, New York. Brother Jones had bought the *New York World*. Just as we reached the dining room door he said: "George, there has been a terrible railroad wreck at Thaxton, Virginia. My! What a list of those killed!" Looking at the list I saw "Cleveland, Tennessee." I snatched the paper from his hand and read, while my blood ran cold: "John M. Hardwick, Cleveland, Tennessee, killed and burned; William Marshall, Cleveland, Tennessee, killed and burned; Willie Steed, Cleveland, Tennessee, killed and burned."

I threw up my hands and said: "O Sam, the next name would have been 'George R. Stuart, Cleveland, Tennessee, killed and burned,' but for the authority of my precious mother."

I ran out to a bulletin board and found when the first train toward home was due. We turned from our journey and came immediately home. I found my little town gathered about the street, and sadness resting like a cloud upon the whole town.

As I walked up the street the mother of one of the boys, in whose home I had boarded in other days (she was almost as a mother to me), ran out in the streets and said, "O George, if I only had the body of my precious boy!"

When I reached the gate I saw my mother come running; she threw her arms around me and said: "Thank God! my boy is safe."

And I said: "Mother, I never missed it when I took your advice. I am sure I shall take it from this to the grave." I found that I had never learned what God meant when He said: "Honor thy father and thy mother; that thy days may be long upon the land which the Lord thy God giveth thee."

Home authority has saved life and it has saved character and saved thousands of souls; for the lack of it the world is going to rot.

My Personal Testimony

I could never tell the amazing influence of my mother on my own life, although she went to Heaven before I was six years old.

Early I got the impression that my mother knew everything, and I was not surprised when, after I was a grown man, I heard her beloved sister, my aunt, say, "Your mother was the smartest woman I ever knew, and the best." Of course she was!

I had sat on the floor by the Singer sewing machine while she pumped the treadle up and down and made her own clothes and those for her children, her husband's shirts and underwear. And I had begged for a little chew of the beeswax with which she waxed her thread. When about four years old I entered into scientific exploration: How far would a round English pea go into my nose? Then I was horrified to find I could not get it out and my wise mother laughed that it was nothing until I quit crying. Then she took me out in the sunshine, had me look at the sun.

Kerchoo! And as I sneezed the pea flew out and we laughed together! And I slept, with my little sister, in a trundle bed which rolled under Mama's and Daddy's bed in the daytime but at night it was taken out and the sides were lifted and made a bed right near her.

My mother loved her babies. Five of us were born by the time she was thirty. And when George was a nursing baby and I was four, I watched the interesting process of his nourishment till Mamma said, "Are you hungry, too?" And I leaned my face against her breast. And I must say that until I was a grown man, a woman's breast simply symbolized motherhood and purity and virtue and loving care, and I never thought of a woman's breast as a matter of sex temptation.

My mother sang and we children gathered around her and sang gospel songs. And once she sang a gospel song of the time seventy years ago, "Turned Away From the Beautiful Gate." And I even remember some of the words:

Turned away from the beautiful gate,
Turned away from the beautiful gate,
In sorrow we'll mourn o'er our sorrowful fate,
Turned away from the beautiful gate.

And though only about five years old I stopped singing and began to weep. What if I should miss Heaven when Mother and all the good people are going? And I remember so well how, when I lied to my mother and she knelt beside me and in deep distress told me how God hated a lie, I wondered if I, who had lied to my mother when I was all dressed for church, I, a preacher's boy—I wondered if God would ever forgive me or if I would have another chance!

Oh, how hard it is for a boy to get away from God if his

mother has bred in him a holy conscience about sin and a holy concern for heavenly things!

And when my mother lay dying, out in the country near Red River in Cooke County, Texas, and we were called in to see her and tell her good-by, she made everybody promise to meet her in Heaven. And then she asked my cousin, "Georgia, will you sing for me?"

And Cousin Georgia asked, "What shall I sing, Aunt Sadie?"

And my mother answered, "Sing 'How firm a foundation, ye saints of the Lord, Is laid for your faith in His excellent Word.' "

And Cousin Georgia played it on the reed organ and in a choked voice she sang it. And my mother lifted her thin hands and there was a heavenly light on her face as she said, "I can see Jesus and my baby now!" Her hands fell across her breast and she was gone and I knew then she had gone to Heaven, just as I know it now.

Oh, the godly influence of a good mother! I mean a mother who is out and out for Christ and says so and is determined to get her children to Heaven and her loved ones saved.

III. WHAT AWFUL THING HAS HAPPENED TO MOTHERHOOD AND CHRISTIAN WOMANHOOD IN AMERICA?

We must face it! We must face it honestly! The American home has declined in godliness and the American mother is not now the overwhelming influence for God and purity and righteousness that once mothers were. Why?

1. The Decline of Religion in the Home

The breakdown in discipline, the forsaking of the family altar, and women breaking away from motherhood as the most blessed career, has lost the American mother her place of influence and power for Christ and righteousness and character. The so-called "generation gap" simply means that fathers and mothers have not maintained their authority, have not punished sin.

The way to stop the increase of crime among youth is to stop raising criminals in the home. Dr. Spock, with his silly teaching about not crossing children, and the Dewey philosophy in education, along with worldliness, and a cowardly pulpit, have raised this generation without respect for authority. That means without respect for the government, the policemen, the teacher; without respect for the law of the land; without respect for the preacher, and so without respect for father and mother, or God!

And the influence of a Christian mother for God must be a decidedly Christian influence. It is not some cheap, emotional attraction which would come naturally from the fact of motherhood. Untrained, undisciplined children, in a home where there is no power of God, no authority of the Bible, no strict accountability for sin—in such a home a Christian mother will have little influence for Christ.

2. America, Obsessed With Emphasis on Sex as a Matter of Animal Enjoyment, a Matter of Lust and Selfish Gratification, Takes Away the Glory From Motherhood

Those godly mothers of the past who wielded such a mighty influence in the home and over husband and children did not wear miniskirts nor shorts nor slacks.

They had long hair and they did not have to have it washed and dyed and set in the beauty parlors every week. They did not read dirty novels, did not smoke cigarettes. They not only did not use four-letter obscene words, but if a boy used a word even a little off-color he might get his mouth washed out with lye soap! And those mothers never allowed a boy or girl to say, "I don't want to!" Or, "I'm not going to do it!" They answered the first time they were spoken to; they got up when they were called; they said, "Yes, ma'am."

They didn't bob their hair, they didn't smoke cigarettes. And do you think those women were to be pitied? They held their husbands with love and respect that rarely wavered and their children later rose up to call them blessed. In our community, I remember we heard that sometimes people did get a divorce but I did not know of any cases and we only knew of one bad woman, immoral, in the whole area!

3. In Those Days People Wanted Children

Oh, how women in Bible times wanted children! So you can understand how Sarah and Rebekah and Rachel and Hannah and Elisabeth and the mother of Samson pleaded with God until He gave them children. And so it has been in the past among godly people. Adam and Eve were commanded to "be fruitful, and multiply, and replenish the earth." And to Noah it was commanded, "And you, be ye fruitful, and multiply; bring forth abundantly in the earth, and multiply therein" (Gen. 9:7).

And Psalm 127:3-5 says, "Lo, children are an heritage of the Lord: and the fruit of the womb is his reward. As arrows are in the hand of a mighty man; so are children of the youth. Happy is the man that hath his quiver full of them: they shall not be ashamed, but they shall speak with the enemies in the gate."

And the blessed one who fears the Lord and walks in His way has the promise, "Thy wife shall be as a fruitful vine by the sides of thine house: thy children like olive plants round about thy table" (Ps. 128:3). In those days, when children were taught to mind, taught to obey, mothers were rarely frantic to get a babysitter and get away and never anxious to see school start so the children would be out from under foot. Oh, a godly mother with well-reared children delights in the presence of her children and they in her.

In the old days there was no silly talk of "population explosion." Good people thought then, as sensible people still believe, there are not too many godly Christian children raised up to serve God in our country.

Bob Jones, great evangelist, was the eleventh child of his mother. Was that too many? John Wesley was the fifteenth child of his mother and Charles the seventeenth. Was that too many? And Susannah Wesley had time to take an hour or so every week for each separate child alone to teach them the Word of God.

A writer in *The Church Herald* wrote:

> "It is generally acknowledged that the Methodist Church had its start with the forming of the 'Holy Club.' But one writer disputes this fact and said it is incorrect. He says, 'The Methodist Church began at Susannah Wesley's knee, when she rocked Charles in a cradle and held John on her lap while she patiently taught him to read, "In the beginning God created the heavens and the earth." ' "

There is good evidence that John Wesley largely got his Arminian and holiness theology from his father, Samuel

Wesley, but his earnest zeal and burning conscience and dedication, he got very largely from his mother. There are not too many children being reared by women like Susannah Wesley!

Now there is a great to-do about "the pill," about contraceptives, about preventing conception. Oh, good women ought to rejoice in the blessing of motherhood! I was thrilled the other day as I talked long distance on a business matter to a woman in a business office and she knew me only casually but she knew, of course, that I love the Lord. Before we started the business matter she said, "Oh, I have the best news for you! I'm going to have a baby!"

This is the way women ought to feel about the blessing of God—an immortal soul put in their care, an opportunity for influence such as a woman might not otherwise have. Now there are all kinds of excuses as to why they want laws repealed against abortion; women want the right to help murder their unborn babies. That kind of women will never have much godly influence.

No, the blatant appeal for a display of sex charms, the patterning after Hollywood wantons, the rebellion against the duties of home and wifehood and motherhood, do not make for godly Christian influence.

Queen Victoria of England was a noble Christian woman. To her son Albert she said, "I want you to make Mother a promise. Promise me that you will read the Bible every day of your life." He promised his mother and when he was king of England he still read the Bible every day according to his vow.

IV. GODLY WOMEN, THIS IS A TIME FOR DEDICATION

I urge everywhere that women take the place God intended, the holy place of godly influence as wives and mothers.

1. Ask God for Children to Rear for Him

If you do not have children, why don't you pray to God and ask Him to give you the privilege of a baby! Again and again I have joined husband and wife in prayer, where doctors had said they could not have children and where the long, empty years had brought only discouragement and failure. And how many times God then gave the child for which they prayed!

So, Elisabeth and Zacharias prayed and God gave John the Baptist; so Hannah prayed and God gave Samuel; so Abraham and Sarah prayed and God gave Isaac, long after it seemed humanly impossible. Pray that God will give you a son to raise for Him. The way to stop having criminals is to quit rearing them. And the way to have preachers and soul winners is to rear them in the home.

2. Make Sure Your Home Is a Place of Family Worship

Every home ought to have prayer at every meal. And every home ought to have a certain time set apart when the whole family reads the Bible together and prays together, a time when they memorize some of the Psalms and other chapters in the Scriptures and many, many verses. Put Christ first in the home. Deuteronomy 6:6-9 says:

"And these words, which I command thee this day, shall

be in thine heart: And thou shalt teach them diligently unto thy children, and shalt talk of them when thou sittest in thine house, and when thou walkest by the way, and when thou liest down, and when thou risest up. And thou shalt bind them for a sign upon thine hand, and they shall be as frontlets between thine eyes. And thou shalt write them upon the posts of thy house, and on thy gates."

Oh, mothers, here is a way to greatness—build the Word of God into your children till they will never get away from it.

3. Make Your Home Your Career!

Every godly woman should think, "My first duty under God is to my husband. I am to love him, honor him, obey him, and make him happy." And her second duty should be to rear godly children, to teach them honor and obedience, and teach them about Christ and get them saved, to grow in them Christian character.

You could work outside the home and make a little more money, but you had better have a less expensive home and less expensive carpets on the floor. You had better do with one bathroom instead of two, and one car instead of two or three, if need be, and have time with your children.

Better time with the children than with too many clubs, and too many concerts, and too many committees.

So, be sure you teach your children the Word of God, be sure that they are with you in church and sit with you in the house of God. Make your home a career. Make it a matter of daily prayer and dedication.

And, oh, dear woman, if you have not been saved, how can you be a good mother? Oh, Mother, if you are unsaved, turn today to Christ and trust Him and have His help in doing your part for a Christian home.

2/ "And Ye Fathers. . ."

"I write unto you, fathers, because ye have known him that is from the beginning."—I John 2:13.

"And, ye fathers, provoke not your children to wrath: but bring them up in the nurture and admonition of the Lord."—Eph. 6:4.

"Like as a father pitieth his children. . . ."—Ps. 103:13.

". . .and the glory of children are their fathers."—Prov. 17:6.

It is natural and good that one should have very sweet memories and a warmth of heart about his mother. My own mother died when I was five years old. What memories I have of her are very sweet. How capable and wise, how tender, how devoted to Christ she was, even as I remember her today and her glorious Home-going. But long years went by when my father was my only parent. So the profound impact of my father upon my character and convictions and happiness was many times that of my mother.

To me, my father was a knight in shining armor! He was wiser than all my teachers. His standards of conduct and integrity were so strong that I had a godly fear lest I should ever disappoint him. It is true that we were sometimes very poor but, strangely enough, we always regarded ourselves as among the leading families where we lived, and indeed my father's opinion had more weight among the people than the opinion of almost anybody else! We were the kind of people, it seemed to all of our family, who never were less than self-supporting, never needed charity. Just as on the school board, or in the church meeting, my father's counsel was always sought by our elders. It was understood that we children would make the best grades in school.

Some five years after my mother died, my father married again a noble, good woman. And what a task she had trying to mother a brood of four so vigorous, so self-contained as we were! But I remember one time when about an incidental matter she doubted my word and said, "I am afraid you are lying to me about that!"—I was shocked beyond measure! How could anybody think that one of our family would tell a lie deliberately!

There is no way for me to tell the impact of my father's character and standards on me and on the rest of the family. We felt it the most natural thing in the world when he was elected to the state legislature, that he was a friend, first of Senator Joe Bailey and later of Governor Pat Neff.

Oh, that every father in America had the standards and character of my own father! How blessed and how blessed of God would this righteous nation then be!

I. HOW BLESSED ARE FATHERS!

Mothers are mentioned in the Bible three hundred and

sixty-three times on my count, but fathers are mentioned five times as often—over thirteen hundred times. God intended the father to be an image of God the Father. He is to be the high priest of his family. He is to be the king and the judge, the counselor, the provider, the avenger of wrong!

God intended the man to be a picture of God. In I Corinthians 11:7 the Scripture says, "For a man indeed ought not to cover his head, forasmuch as he is the image and glory of God: but the woman is the glory of the man." God is just saying that a woman is given long hair as a veiling, a covering, a reminder and picture of submission to her husband and father. Yes, that Scripture says that if a woman have long hair, it is a glory to her, but if a man have long hair, it is a shame to him. For there is nobody between a man and Christ Jesus. So the man is not to wear long hair. Men take off their hats in church. So the man represents God in a particular sense that women and children do not, The pronouns about God in the Bible are *He* and *His* and *Him*.

So when Jesus taught us to pray, He said we should say, "Our Father, which art in heaven." And describing the tender, loving care of God, the psalmist said, "Like as a father pitieth his children, so the Lord pitieth them that fear him" (Ps. 103:3).

In the Bible the term "the fatherless" describes those of utter helplessness. If a mother died, there would be great emotional loss, but a child would still have a home, still have support, still have authority and protection. Not so with a child who lost his father.

Oh, it is something blessed and enormously important for one to be a father. And what a privilege it is that God allows a man to become a father, to be a partner with Him in creation of an immortal soul and a little personality in a body.

In Bible times the father was understood to be the high priest, who offered sacrifices for his family, as did Abraham and Job and others. God had Abraham to prepare to offer his son Isaac as a sacrifice, though we are not told that Sarah, the mother, was even consulted. Jephthah vowed to offer the one who came to meet him after a victorious battle, and it was his daughter. In Deuteronomy 21:18-21, a father, with the consent of the mother, could condemn a rebellious and drunken son to death by stoning.

In Bible times a father often acted as a prophet of God. So it was when Noah pronounced a curse and blessings on his three sons, in Genesis 9:24-27. He spoke for God. So it was when Isaac, old and blind, and yet with the Spirit of God upon him, gave a blessing to Jacob and a lesser blessing to Esau, in Genesis 27:26-40. Jacob, before he died, had all his sons to gather at his bedside and he pronounced prophesies on each of them, as we see in Genesis 49.

And that prophetic role of husband and father is hinted at again in I Corinthians 14:34 and 35 where the command is, "Let your women keep silence in the churches: for it is not permitted unto them to speak; but they are commanded to be under obedience, as also saith the law. And if they will learn anything, let them ask their husbands at home: for it is a shame for women to speak in the church."

There has been a sad erosion in America of the authority and honor and the responsibility which fathers have borne in the past. Once a father approved or disapproved the marriage of sons as well as daughters, and oftentimes arranged it. A father sometimes apprenticed out his son in a certain trade to prepare him for his life's work. But many things have tended to take away from the glory and authority of fathers. The feminist movement, the rebellion of wives, the giving the right of women to vote have all minimized the role of the father. Godless psychologists have taught that corporal punishment of children is wrong, that every teen-ager should plan his own life—for or against drugs and alcohol and tobacco and sex immorality—as he likes. Politicians have hoped to get the vote of the radical left by giving the vote to teen-agers. So God's place for fathers as high priest of a family, as judge and ruler and provider and guide, has been eroded all for the worse in America.

Oh, but we should remember that in God's plan, fathers are the glory of their children.

II. CHILDREN FOLLOW THEIR FATHERS

Children are very largely what the fathers make them. It is true that mothers are with younger children more perhaps than the father. And a mother's influence is strong. Why is it the song says, "Mother's prayers have followed me"? And a prodigal is pictured as saying, "Tell Mother I'll be there"? I think that the influence of a mother's prayers are tremendous, but the prodigal more often becomes one because he did not have a strong father to discipline and rule him.

So it was with the sons of Eli. Since discipline is more likely left in the hands of the father, and the blessed promise is, "Train up a child in the way he should go; and when he is old, he will not depart from it," it seems likely that when a father is what he ought to be, his son does not turn out to be a prodigal, but will turn to Christ.

Many a Christian woman, married to an unsaved man,

learns with distress that the children follow the wicked father after awhile instead of her, the devoted mother. Children do more generally follow their fathers, and we think in every case there is a strong impact of the father's influence on the child.

There is the influence of inherited taint of sin. Cain, when he slew his brother, was simply manifesting a part of the death that came to Adam and part of the nature that he inherited from a fallen father and mother. And David, grieving over his sins, admitted that he was brought forth in iniquity, that he inherited it from birth. And God has promised, "The Lord is longsuffering, and of great mercy, forgiving iniquity and transgression, and by no means clearing the guilty, visiting the iniquity of the fathers upon the children unto the third and fourth generation" (Num. 14:18). Not that God will punish the children for the sins of the father but that the children inherit the sins of the father.

Children more often follow the sinful example of their fathers than follow evil instructions. Even wicked fathers usually want their children to be good. The drunkard does not want his son to be a drunkard. But an old proverb says, "What you are talks so loud I can't hear what you say." So a father's influence for sin is worse in his life than his words. See how David's children followed him in sin. It is true that David was a godly man. He was even called a man after God's own heart. Of his devotion, his prayerfulness, and the Spirit of God often upon him, one cannot doubt.

But David was trapped into sin—adultery with another man's wife. Then because he was king, he could order Uriah into a battle where he would be killed.

It seems likely that the children came to know about

their father's sin. Or if they did not know the sin, yet there was some subtle weakness that influenced them to go the same way. So Amnon raped his half sister, Tamar. Her brother Absalom brooded two years, then murdered Amnon. Then perhaps unforgiven and held at arm's length too long by David, Absalom betrayed his father, won away the hearts of the people and led in a rebellion and would have killed his father, and he himself was killed in the great battle. Oh, children do follow their fathers!

Another illustration of that is of the kings, Asa and Jehoshaphat. As we read the story in II Chronicles 14, Asa was a great and good king in Judah. "And Asa did that which was good and right in the eyes of the Lord his God: For he took away the altars of the strange gods, and the high places, and brake down the images, and cut down the groves" (vss. 2,3). He carried on the revival throughout the fenced cities of Judah.

Against Asa came Zerah, the Ethiopian, who had a million soldiers and three hundred chariots. They cried to God and God spared the small army and destroyed the mighty army of the Ethiopians in answer to prayer. Then Asa went further with the reforms and revival. Asa and the people were warned by their prophet Azariah, and ". . .when Asa heard these words, and the prophecy of Obed the prophet, he took courage, and put away the abominable idols out of all the land of Judah and Benjamin, and out of the cities which he had taken from mount Ephraim, and renewed the altar of the Lord, that was before the porch of the Lord" (vs. 8). "And they entered into a covenant to seek the Lord God of their fathers with all their heart and with all their soul" (vs. 12).

But trouble threatened—the king of Israel in the north arose against Jehoshaphat and he took gold from the

Temple of the Lord and bribed Ben-hadad, king of Syria, to attack Israel, the northern tribes, and thus free him from the threat. "And at that time Hanani the seer came to Asa king of Judah, and said unto him, Because thou hast relied on the king of Syria, and not relied on the Lord thy God, therefore is the host of the king of Syria escaped out of thine hand" (II Chron. 16:7). And Hanani reminded him of how God had wonderfully helped and how God was looking everywhere "to shew himself strong in the behalf of them whose heart is perfect toward him." And Hanani said, "Herein thou hast done foolishly: therefore from henceforth thou shalt have wars" (vs. 9). And Asa, the good man, imprisoned Hanani and others for his warning.

Time went on. Jehoshaphat succeeded to the throne. "And the Lord was with Jehoshaphat, because he walked in the first ways of his father David, and sought not unto Baalim; But sought to the Lord God of his father, and walked in his commandments, and not after the doings of Israel" (II Chron. 17:3). So there was a great revival and he sent Levites everywhere to preach the Gospel and teach the book of the law. So God continued blessing Jehoshaphat, as we read in II Chronicles 17.

But Ahab became king in the northern kingdom and the 18th chapter tells us how "Jehoshaphat had riches and honour in abundance, and joined affinity with Ahab." He went to visit Ahab and "Ahab king of Israel said unto Jehoshaphat king of Judah, Wilt thou go with me to Ramoth-gilead? And he answered him, I am as thou art, and my people as thy people; and we will be with thee in the war."

They went to the war against Syria despite the warning of God's prophet. Ahab was killed. The northern army was scattered. Jehoshaphat came home. And there in II

Chronicles 19:1-3 he had a serious warning from a seer, Jehu. Now Jehu was the son of Hanani the prophet that had also rebuked Jehoshaphat's father Asa. Jehu said to King Jehoshaphat, ". . .Shouldest thou help the ungodly, and love them that hate the Lord? therefore is wrath upon thee from before the Lord" (II Chron. 19:2). Jehoshaphat went on serving the Lord, but he had compromised seriously. He followed the same sin of Asa his father. But Jehu the prophet followed the example of his godly father Hanani. Both prophets were faithful to the Lord, both the kings compromised, the one following the other.

But the lesson is not ended. For when Jehoshaphat died his son Jehoram came to the throne. Ahab also had a son Jehoram reigning in Israel. Did Jehoshaphat name his son after the older son of his friend Ahab? Perhaps so. Jehoshaphat had sold out to Jehoram as he had to Ahab. And now Jehoram, when he followed his father Jehoshaphat, married Ahab's daughter and went in the ways of Ahab and the wicked idolaters.

The son followed the father. A little compromise leads to a big compromise. When one sows to the wind, he reaps the whirlwind. Children follow their fathers.

III. THE MIGHTY POWER OF A FATHER'S GODLY TEACHING AND EXAMPLE

God's people are commanded to teach the children diligently the Word of God, to talk about it when they rise up and when they sit down, when they walk by the way. They are to write the Word of God on the walls of the houses and on their gates and carry it before their eyes and in their hands, says Deuteronomy 6:6-9.

One man who seems to have done that was Jonadab of

the family of Rechab. What a story we read about the Rechabites in the days of Jeremiah!

As a lesson to Israel, to show how far they had gone into idolatry and sin and how they had failed to follow God's commandments, God had Jeremiah offer to the men of the house of Rechab wine to drink. And we read in Jeremiah 35:3-10:

"Then I took Jaazaniah the son of Jeremiah, the son of Habaziniah, and his brethren, and all his sons, and the whole house of the Rechabites; And I brought them into the house of the Lord, into the chamber of the sons of Hanan, the son of Igdaliah, a man of God, which was by the chamber of the princes, which was above the chamber of Maaseiah the son of Shallum, the keeper of the door: And I set before the sons of the house of the Rechabites pots full of wine, and cups, and I said unto them, Drink ye wine. But they said, We will drink no wine: for Jonadab the son of Rechab our father commanded us, saying, Ye shall drink no wine, neither ye, nor your sons for ever: Neither shall ye build house, nor sow seed, nor plant vineyard, nor have any: but all your days ye shall dwell in tents; that ye may live many days in the land where ye be strangers. Thus have we obeyed the voice of Jonadab the son of Rechab our father in all that he hath charged us, to drink no wine all our days, we, our wives, our sons, nor our daughters; Nor to build houses for us to dwell in: neither have we vineyard, nor field, nor seed: But we have dwelt in tents, and have obeyed, and done according to all that Jonadab our father commanded us."

And nearly two hundred years before Jonadab had given instruction to his people to avoid wine. They had taken that much to heart. Fathers had taught it to sons. And they were not to set their hearts on the things of this world, nor to live in the wickedness of the city. And they had obeyed!

Oh, for the influence of a godly father upon his children!

How much of that influence of a father is intangible, even. I look back to my boyhood. Our home, a simple home but a hospitable one, was always open to preachers. When a man of God came to our community or to preach in the little church in our town, how often they would come as guests at our home! I had the privilege of unharnessing the preacher's horse and feeding and watering him. And then after supper the preacher and my father would often talk long into the night. They told blessed tales of revival, of wonderful conversions, of answer to prayer. They talked about the things of God. And there would come a time when the children of the household were supposed to go to bed. But I would sometimes sit as quietly as possible, so as not to be noticed, in a corner of the room or behind the chairs of the adults and listen to the wonderful conversation. Oh, how wonderful it seemed to me to know God's dealings with His people! So the things of God were planted in my heart.

Much of the influence of my father was an intangible thing that perhaps could not well be described. My father named me for two Baptist preachers, friends whom he loved. After he had gone to Heaven, I found in an old, old Bible belonging to my father those words which Zacharias spoke of the baby John the Baptist when he was born, "His name is John" deeply underlined. And I knew that my father, who named me after preachers and who named me John as "a man sent from God," wanted me to be a preacher.

At our house we went to church every time the church doors opened. We all went to Sunday school. All of us, adults and all, went to the B.Y.P.U., the young people's meeting. We all went to Wednesday night prayer meeting if they had prayer meeting. When they had revival services we went to the weekday morning services as well as the night. We went when there was plowing to be done. We went in the midst of harvest. We went when it rained or snowed. One had to be mighty sick at our house to miss the church service. And rather than words, some of that spoke to our hearts about how spiritual things were first and God wanted first place in our lives. Some way it was understood from the time we were little children that we would tithe, and we did. Oh, the blessed influence of a godly father!

There were things in my father's life that shined through year after year.

When my father was a young preacher, he went to Louisville, Kentucky, for a year at the Southern Baptist Theological Seminary. And during that time he was a student pastor at a little Baptist church in a small town, I think in Campbellsville, Kentucky. It was about 1890. Once he started to the church where he would preach on a winter's morning. As he walked by a lumber yard, he saw a drunken man lying on the snowy ground where he had fallen, unable to walk. He spoke to some men about him! They scoffed at him. "It will do no good to help him. He is drunk all the time. There is no use to bother about him. Others have tried and couldn't do any good." But my father was afraid the man would die from exposure. He lifted the man up and helped to get him home. They helped undress him and cover him and give him hot coffee until the shivering limbs were warmed. They called a doctor to wait on the man. Then he went back a little later when the man was more sober and went again until he won the man to Christ. This drunkard made a good, sober Christian.

More than thirty years later a man came from Kentucky to Texas looking for a preacher named Will Rice. That father, saved years ago, had lived a good Christian life, then on his deathbed he told his children again of the man who had saved his life and then won him to Christ and helped to make him a decent citizen, a godly father and husband. He said to an older son, "If you get a chance to see that man in Texas, tell him that I lived for God and died in the faith and went gladly to Heaven. Tell him that in Heaven I will wait for him."

So the son looked forward to the time when he could see and thank the man who had won his father. He got to be passenger agent for a railroad. He traveled as he wished. He came to Gainesville, Texas, where had been the home of my father. He inquired there and they told him, "He lives now in Decatur, Texas." So he came to Decatur and looked up my father to thank him for blessings long ago.

I cannot tell how the godly influence of my father, not only his teaching but his example, not only certain acts that I noted but the general influence of his heart in doing right, in looking out for others, his moral integrity and his spiritual devotion, has influenced my life.

IV. CHILDREN ARE OFTEN BLESSED OF GOD FOR THEIR FATHER'S SAKE

How often we find statements like this in the Bible: God blessed Rehoboam for David his father's (his ancestor's) sake. When Jehoram went wrong, God would not take the kingdom of Judah from him for David's sake.

Oh, a son may be blessed for his father's sake!

I grew up in the cattle country of West Texas. The village school had sometimes only two and sometimes three teachers for all the grades, from first grade through high school. So we had no high school graduation. We went as long as there was something to be learned. And then I got books and studied and took a teacher's examination, got a second grade teacher's certificate, then I studied more and went back to the county seat and took examinations and got a first-class teacher's certificate.

When I first went to Archer City, Texas, the county seat, to take my teacher's examination, when the morning session was done I found waiting for me Judge Walker, a prominent, good man. He must take me to his home. His horse and buggy were waiting. I felt embarrassed, but nothing would do but that I should go for the noon meal at his home. I went. And the judge insisted I must make this my home these two or three days I was to be in Archer City. I protested but the family would not take no for an answer.

It was a lovely home. The table linen was so white and the silver gleamed, and the manners in the household were beautiful. I was not accustomed to such luxury. And the judge must personally drive me to and from the courthouse for every session! Nothing was too good for me.

I was grateful, but I wondered. I did not know till later why the judge had taken me to his heart and so wonderfully cared for the rather naive and poor country boy.

But I learned the secret. Once my father had been in Wichita Falls and there he saw on the street a tramp, a bum, with unkempt beard and shaggy hair and dirty clothes. My father recognized him. He said, "Bruce Walker, what are you doing here!" And Bruce told a sad tale. He had gone to Wichita Falls for a brief time. He had gotten drunk and spent his money. And then his clothes were so soiled he could not get a job. He slept in alleys. He got a handout where he could. He was ashamed to go back home, not wanting his distinguished father and his cultured sister to see him as a poor bum.

My father took him to a barber shop where he had a bath and a shave and a haircut. He took him to a clothing store and bought new clothes for him. He took him to the railroad station and got a ticket for him and put him on the train to go back to his father in Archer City.

The months went by, and Judge Walker had a chance to do for my father's son a little bit in appreciation for what my father had done for his poor, prodigal boy.

Oh, children get many blessings from God because of their godly fathers!

After my father died, my brother Bill lived for a time in West Texas with my sister who taught school there. He decided to go back to Decatur to college. He had no money. He rode his gray mare. The miles were long. He had no money to buy food. He would expect to sleep somewhere in a haystack at night. Maybe somewhere he could get a handout. As he rode along he became rather bitter. He had tried to live right. He had tried to listen to his father's instructions. It did not seem to have paid off. What would he do?

He rode on without the noonday meal. As evening approached the sky grew dark with clouds. It was going to rain. He stopped at a house beside the road and called. A man came to the door. My brother said, "It is going to rain. Could I sleep in your barn tonight?"

The man said yes if he would not smoke, would not use matches, he could sleep in the barn. Then the man said, "What is your name?" And he answered, "My name is Bill Rice. I am going to Decatur to college."

The man said, "Rice? Rice? Are you any kin to the late Senator Will Rice from Decatur?"

"Yes," Bill said. "I am his son." The man immediately called his wife. "Set the supper back on the table. Here is the son of Will Rice! I want you to meet him." He unsaddled the mare and fed her. They washed on the back porch and Bill sat down to a good supper. A bed was made for him on the front porch in the dry. Before they slept this godly man prayed and thanked God they got to meet the son of Will Rice.

The next morning he woke Bill up early. Breakfast was ready. He would want to get on his way. Before they left he told Bill a story.

Years before in hard times he had been about to lose his farm. He couldn't raise any money. The mortgage was about to be foreclosed. And my father had gone to the bank and arranged for a loan. The farm was saved. Then my father had taken time to tell the man he needed more help than money. He needed Jesus Christ. The man and his wife were saved. They had raised godly children and they had all gotten farms nearby. Now how glad he was to do something for the son of Will Rice who had helped him so greatly years before!

Oh, I say, children are often blessed for the sake of their fathers!

And just so it is that all of us have a thousand blessings that could be charged to the sweet influence of our elder Brother, our Saviour, the Lord Jesus Christ.

Fathers, you are somebody. You have a blessed responsibility. You are the high priest of your home. You represent God Almighty. So I beg you, in Jesus' dear name, make sure your household lives for God and that your children can be so taught, so disciplined and so prayed over that they will serve the Lord.

3/ *"Home, Sweet Home"*

The Dearest Place on Earth, the Nearest Place to Heaven Is a Happy Christian Home

Home can be almost a hell on earth. The week before this was written, in Dallas a man came to the home of his estranged wife with a shotgun. She pleaded in vain for her life, then turned and ran. The full charge of shot hit her in the back and she fell, dead. Then the man put the muzzle of the gun to his mouth and blew away the whole side of his face and fell mortally wounded, was carried to the hospital and died without regaining consciousness. That proves, I think, that home can be almost a hell on earth.

In my home county one year there were three-fourths as many divorces as there were marriage licenses. In three out of every four homes, marriage failed, dissension, jealousy, suspicion or even hate turned the marital cup into gall and the air castles of love into ashes. Drinking, unfaithfulness, brutality and desertion played their part in these home tragedies. And only God knows how many homes were miserable besides those dissolved in divorce. Some couples applied for divorces and did not get them, other homes are held together for the sake of children and some wives endure their husbands for financial support and some husbands keep their wives to avoid scandal. Certain it is that homes are not always happy homes. Homes can be failures, places where families endure but do not enjoy each other. Sometimes family ties are little more than a convenience. Often homes are little hells on earth.

But home was not so intended. The good God who instituted marriage and the family, provided that homes should be a blessing and joy; a refuge of peace and happiness, a haven from trouble, strife and sorrow. God intended that home should be "the dearest place on earth, the nearest place to Heaven."

The First Home in the Garden of Eden

Little as we think about it, the institution of the home, marriage and family was meant for perfect people in a paradise of beauty! Home was intended to be the last step to perfect happiness in a lovely and sinless world. God made Adam, the first man, perfect and holy, in His own image. And then, even in the Garden of Eden God said, "It is not good that the man should be alone; I will make him an help meet for him" (Gen. 2:18). So God made a woman and brought her to the man and Adam loved her and she was his wife. Thus God Himself in the Garden of Eden founded the first home. It was the last step needed for perfect happiness on earth in the paradise of God.

After that time the curse of sin entered in and Adam and his wife became sinners and all their descendants are cursed with the taint of sin. Every man and every woman in the world is a poor fallen creature, and nature itself bears the marks of the curse that came with sin. The world has become a place of war and crime and hate and rebellion against God and unnameable wickedness and violence. Yet when the angels with a flaming sword drove Adam and Eve from the Garden of Eden, they brought part of the paradise with them. The loving mercy of God provided that the outcasts from Eden should take with them the Edenic blessing of marriage and love and home! Every home, then, is a part of the Garden of Eden. Every home is meant to be a heaven on earth. Every home should be a refuge from a sin-cursed world all about us and a likeness of our heavenly home which God has prepared for them that love Him.

The Christian Home Depends on a Christian Marriage

Happiness in the home depends on having God there, and having the home honor Christ. Only where Christ is Lord can happiness have full place. If we expect to have a little bit of Heaven in our home, then we must have Christ there and His will must be done. Sin brings trouble and heartache. It always has, it always will. Sin broke up the Garden of Eden. Sin has brought death into the world. Every sickness, every failure, all the trouble and misunderstanding and heartbreak of the world has been brought in by sin. So the only way to have a really happy, blessed home is to have a Christian home, a home where the principals to the marriage are saved people who put Christ first.

It is dangerous and foolish for a Christian to marry one who is not saved.

Can Christ and Satan both be Lord in the same house? Can you mix Hell in with Heaven, and still make the home happy? When a Christian marries a child of Satan, can one expect their union, the most intimate of all human relationships, to be a happy one? No, no! The marriage of a Christian to an unsaved person is a sin against God, and the certain result is misery and unhappiness.

I have often seen, as you have, the happy case where God has answered the tearful prayers of a wife for her unsaved husband, or of a husband for his unsaved wife. Sometimes after many years prayer has been answered and the loved one, married years ago in defiance of the plain command of God (a sinful marriage it was), is saved. God's mercy is great. God is willing to forgive sin. Yet every pastor knows, every evangelist knows, that the most frequent and heartbreaking failure of an answer to prayer is that of a wife praying for her husband whom she married in sin and contrary to the command of God. Many times such are never saved or are saved after much suffering and trouble in the home. A Christian who marries an unbeliever sins against God and makes sure of trouble.

In II Corinthians 6:14-18 God's Word says:

"Be ye not unequally yoked together with unbelievers: for what fellowship hath righteousness with unrighteousness? and what communion hath light with darkness? And what concord hath Christ with Belial? or what part hath he that believeth with an infidel? And what agreement hath the temple of God with idols? for ye are the temple of the living God; as God hath said, I will dwell in them, and walk in them; and I will be their God, and they shall be my people. Wherefore come out from among them, and be ye separate, saith the Lord, and touch not the unclean thing; and I will receive you. And will be a Father unto you, and ye shall be my sons, and daughters, saith the Lord Almighty."

Righteousness with unrighteousness is mismated, light mated with darkness is sin. Christ does not have concord with Belial. He that believeth should not have part with an infidel (literally an unbeliever). The temple of God (the Christian's body) is not at agreement with idols. Therefore, the command of God is, "Come out from among them, and be ye separate, saith the Lord, and touch not the unclean. . ." (The word "thing" is not in the original. God does not mean an unclean thing, but an unclean person) ". . .and I will receive you, and will be a Father unto you and ye shall be my sons and daughters, saith the Lord Almighty."

If home is to be "the dearest place on earth, the nearest place to Heaven," it must be a place where there is harmony between husband and wife, harmony about the deepest things, the highest things, the noblest things. In other words, Christ must rule in both hearts or there can be no Heaven in the home.

And let me say here that human love, however high and lofty it is, cannot guarantee happiness in the home. Here in America we are wont to think that love is the sum of all that is necessary to make a marriage successful and happy. But it is not true. I have known cases—and you have too—where drunkenness, nagging brutality, incompatability, dissension and disagreement about the holiest things in life came in homes where love was truly present. An unsaved man's love for his wife will not give him a good heart. An unsaved man's love for his wife may not be able to conquer the demon of thirst for drink. An unsaved woman's love for husband will not always make her willing to give up the habits and thoughts and plans of a lifetime. Human love is not sufficient to guarantee happiness in the home.

Do you suppose that in three cases out of four of the marriages that took place in my home county one year;

there was no true love? Three-fourths of the marriages are ending with divorce. Three-fourths of the marriages go on the rocks. That does not mean that human love was not truly present. Men and women who could not live together in peace have often told me they still loved each other. It simply means that if happiness is to reign in the home, there must be something beyond carnal, human love.

Human love cannot regenerate the human heart. Human love does not make one Christlike. Sin abides in the heart that only has human love as a motive. And sin brings trouble anytime, anywhere it appears. Happiness, even in Heaven, would be spoiled if sin were admitted to work its havoc. So home can be happy in proportion as Christ is Lord and as both husband and wife put their dependence on God, love Him first in their lives. Therefore, it is folly for a Christian to marry one who is unsaved. God plainly commands, "Be ye not unequally yoked together with unbelievers."

In Rhome, Texas, some years ago, I preached on this subject. The next day a little woman came to me and laughingly said, "I know what you preached about last night, even if I was not here, and I do not believe it!"

"I think you surely must be mistaken. If you know what I preached, you would surely agree with it, for it is in the Bible," I said. "Read this Scripture with me."

So I turned to II Corinthians 6:14-18 and she read it over. Her face became grave, and before she read through the passage, tears flooded her eyes. Weeping, she turned to me and said, "I didn't know it was in the Bible! I didn't know it was there! Why didn't some preacher tell me this fifteen years ago?"

I knew what caused her tears and her broken heart. She had married an unsaved man. Her fourteen-year-old son, following in the footsteps of his wicked father, was now breaking her heart. Just a child he was, yet she could not get him to attend services, could not get him interested in the things of God. He preferred to follow his father. She was reaping what she sowed.

So I feel my responsibility to you young people. I beg you, do not, if you are a Christian, marry an unsaved person. To do so is to sin against God. To do so means certain trouble and heartache. No human quality of character can guarantee a happy home. Human love cannot bring happiness. Only the blessing of God can make the home happy. For your mate choose only one who knows the Lord Jesus and is willing to put Him first in heart and life.

Solomon, the man greatly loved of God and given wisdom as no other human being ever had, sinned in this matter. Nehemiah said, in rebuking Israelites who after the captivity had sinned by marrying into the heathen people, "Did not Solomon, king of Israel, sin by these things? Yet among many nations was there no king like him who was beloved of his God, and God made him king over all Israel: nevertheless even him did outlandish women cause to sin." Marriage with unsaved women caused even Solomon, the wisest man who ever lived, to sin. Such ungodly marriages bring the displeasure of God. They many times forfeit His blessings upon the home.

If you have committed this sin, then beg God to forgive you. You cannot undo your marriage, and you ought not. The Scripture plainly commanded in such places that, "If any brother hath a wife that believeth not, and she be pleased to dwell with him, let him not put her away" (I Cor. 7:12). Divorce is not the remedy for this wrong. Two wrongs do not make a right. Any marriage recognized by men is now binding in the sight of God. Your sin is of the past. All you can do now is to beg God to forgive you and to undo as far as possible, the wrong and harm that has been wrought by your sin.

But to you who have not committed this sin yet, I beg you, beware! Any person who marries one of the Devil's children is certain to have trouble with his father-in-law, Satan! No home can be happy until Christ is the Lord of the home, the King in the hearts of both man and woman. Success, and happiness, and peace in any other kind of a home is only relative, only a fraction of what it could be if Christ had His way in the hearts of both husband and wife.

Some wife, perhaps, reads this message who has an unhappy home: your husband is unsaved, or less frequently, some husband will read it whose wife is unsaved. May I say to you kindly, you can never expect real spiritual happiness in your home without Christ in the hearts of those who make the home.

If your loved one is unsaved, then today is the day to do your best. If possible, get that husband today to trust in Christ as Saviour. Make your home united around Jesus Christ. That is the only hope for happiness. Or if you who read this are unsaved, you are the fly in the ointment in your home. If you are unsaved in a home where others are Christians, then you are the serpent in the Garden of Eden. "There is no peace, saith my God, to the wicked" (Isa. 57:21). Your home cannot be fully happy without Christ. Turn to Christ today and make your home happy with His presence.

Little Children Needed in a Happy Home

In the Garden of Eden God founded the first home. A happy paradise it was! There, we are told, "God blessed them and God said unto them, Be fruitful, and multiply and replenish the earth, and subdue it" (Gen. 1:28). Even if man had not sinned, God planned that the family should have children. And after sin had brought the wreck of the whole world, and God had swept away civilization in the flood, God repeated the same command to Noah in Genesis 9:1: "And God blessed Noah and his sons, and said unto them, Be fruitful and multiply, and replenish the earth."

I know that there are some homes that cannot have children. God does not always give the blessed privilege of motherhood and fatherhood to men and women in marriage. But in Bible times, barrenness was regarded as a calamity. If you hear the pleading prayer of Hannah, the long continued supplication of Sarah, the way Isaac interceded for his wife, Rebekah, the jealous competition between Leah and Rachel, the joy of the aged Zacharias and Elisabeth when the angel promised the birth of John the Baptist, you know that according to Bible standards, children are essential to the fullest happiness in the home. "As arrows are in the hand of the mighty man; so are children of the youth. Happy is the man that hath his quiver full of them" (Ps. 127:4, 5).

Let modern women be more concerned, if they must, about their schoolgirl complexion, and their girlish form. The painting of the nails, eye make-up, lipstick and permanent waves—these may be the highest themes of thought and ambition of many modern women. But let us be sure that these never did satisfy a heart nor make the home happy.

It is said that while children are little, they trample upon your toes, and when they are grown, they trample upon your heart. I suppose that is true for most people. Well, then, let us have them trampling on our toes and if it must be, let us have them trampling upon our hearts, but God deliver us from an old age without children.

Women had better learn to fear, as Bible women did, barren lives, fruitless wombs, and breasts that never gave suck. God has granted me that, after all the sorrows and toil and gray hair the children may have brought, I yet rejoice to hold my grandchildren in my arms and see my children grown and happy and prosperous in the blessing of God, serving their fellowman and giving their testimony for Christ!

Children cost! Certainly they cost—from the heaviness of the mother and the pangs of childbirth, on down to the burdens of their adulthood. But children, rightly raised, reared in the fear of God, saved by His grace, trained and admonished in His Word—such children are worth all they cost, and more!

I know homes that are never happy. Wives spend money and time, depending upon form and skin and clothes and hair-dressing and jewels, to hold the love of husbands. What they need is one little mutual body they can love and handle and train, one little mind they can enlighten. Homes would not be so easily broken if they had a real tie of flesh and blood. A man and wife whose blood has mingled in the veins of their offspring will not so quickly separate. Those who have watched beside the same little sickbed, have prayed together and had their prayers answered as they listened so carefully to the doctor's verdict, have something that will hold them together as they override many storms of a nagging tongue, neglect or abuse. I advise every husband and wife who can do so to have children, particularly if they are Christians and fit to rear children.

May I say that part of the grief and sin and violence and

wickedness that is coming upon this old world at the present time is to be blamed on the so-called Christian homes. The homes of the poor, the unlettered, the shiftless, continue to multiply. In the homes of college graduates, well-bred, well-trained, cultivated people, children are scarce. If the men and women best fitted to be fathers and mothers have large families of children reared in the nurture and admonition of the Lord, our civilization would have salt enough to keep it from the destruction that is threatening it today. Only eternity can tell how preachers' children have blessed the world. Why should the man who develops only his muscles have more children than the man who develops his mind and character? Some homes can be happy if, in the will of God, He sees fit to withhold the blessings of children. But all who can have children, we believe, should do so, and that home reaches its highest and fullest joy when Father and Mother and children together please God and give their best to Him.

Discipline and Authority in the Home

There can be no happiness without authority. The kingdom of Christ can never come on earth until His will is done here as it is in Heaven. Only when rebellion came in was man cast outside the garden, a fallen soul. No home can be happy without authority.

Here is the basis of all sin: rebellion against authority. The reason for all the crimes against society is this one thing—rebellion against authority.

We spoke at the county jail one Sunday afternoon. Four hundred sixty-five men and women were there. Every one of them, however diverse were their crimes, came there because they rebelled against authority. Every man in the penitentiary goes there for that very reason. Every person in Hell goes there primarily because he rebels against the authority of God and refuses to obey His commands, refuses to trust God's Son, refuses to surrender to His will. We must remember, "The powers that be are ordained of God." God demands obedience to law, obedience to authority.

In the home that must be true, if you are to have the blessing of God and peace, if home is to be a little bit of Heaven upon earth. Rebellion means crime and sin, and these always bring unhappiness. For this reason God has provided that the wife should be subject to her husband. He said to Eve, just outside the Garden of Eden, "Thy desire shall be to thy husband, and he shall rule over thee." And so in the New Testament even, women are commanded to be in subjection to and under obedience to their own husbands (Eph. 5:22, 23; I Pet. 3:1, 6; Titus 2:5).

How necessary, then, that the children God gives a home should be under authority! God commanded Abraham, and confided His plans to Abraham because, He said, "For I know him, that he will command his children and his household after him, and they shall keep the way of the Lord, to do justice and judgment; that the Lord may bring upon Abraham that which he hath spoken of him" (Gen. 18: 19). Eli, in the days of the baby Samuel, was a devout and godly man. Yet upon him and his whole posterity there came the curse of God, "because his sons made themselves vile, and he restrained them not" (I Sam. 3:13). God said that Eli, in not controlling his children, "honourest thy sons above me" (I Sam. 2:29).

This matter of discipline in the home is one of the cardinal doctrines in the Bible. So strict was God's plan about it that Father and Mother were commanded to see their son stoned if he were rebellious and would not hearken unto them. Deuteronomy 21:18-21 says that rebellion in the home is counted as one of the sins worthy of death, along with murder, rape and kidnaping!

You recall that "honour thy father and thy mother" is one of the Ten Commandments which compose all the law of God. Fathers and mothers are commanded to "chasten" the son, and if he is still rebellious and will not heed and becomes a drunkard and a glutton, a rebel, he is to be counted an enemy of society and executed.

So important is this matter of the discipline of children that in the New Testament it is plainly forbidden that a man should be bishop or pastor of a church if he has children accused of riot or are unruly (I Tim. 3:1-5). Again, of one who is to be a pastor it is required that he be one "having his children in subjection with all gravity; (For if a man know not how to rule his own house, how shall he take care of the church of God?) (I Tim. 3: 4, 5).

Do you believe in whipping children? The Bible is as clear on that as it can possibly be. Turn with me to Proverbs 13:24.

"He that spareth his rod hateth his son: but he that loveth him chasteneth him betimes."

True parental love must demand discipline. The parent who does not love his child enough to punish him for sin, encourages a career of wickedness that must bring unhappiness and perhaps ruin. Do not spare the rod, you who love your children. Chastisement goes with love, according to the Word of God.

Again we have the plain command in Proverbs 19:18:

"Chasten thy son while there is hope, and let not thy soul spare for his crying."

I have known some parents who never crossed their children except just enough to make them angry. My father had a way of whipping until we cried and then whipping until we quit crying! Brother, if you expect to be honored in your old age, and expect your children to rise up and call you blessed, then "chasten thy son while there is hope." One day, when he is out from under your thumb and will not listen to you, it may be too late, but while there is hope, chasten him! To hear some modern educators talk, one would suppose that to leave stripes upon the body of a child were a terrible offense. But the Word of God says,

"The blueness of a wound cleanseth away evil: so do stripes the inward parts of the belly."—Prov. 20:30.

Stripes on the back in time, save many a wound in the heart later for the child that you love.

Many people believe that everything depends upon chance; that no one can know definitely how their children will turn out. Sometimes people say to the preacher, "You may talk now, but you never know how it will be with your own children." Well, at least I know that God has promised this: "Train up a child in the way he should go: and when he is old, he will not depart from it" (Prov. 22:6).

As a pastor of a country church years ago, I preached on the subject of a Christian home. One man, a member of the church, came to me with a good deal of indignation and said, "Pastor, you must go home with me." At his insistence I finally excused myself from others with whom I had agreed to visit, and went to his home. There he said to me, "Pastor, I do not believe what you preached this morning. It simply isn't so!"

I answered back, "What did I preach that isn't so?"

He said, "It is simply not true that if you train a boy right, he will not leave the right way after he is grown. I know I did raise my boy right!"

After a good deal of inquiry, he finally sadly admitted to me that his boy was in the Texas Penitentiary at Huntsville. I said to him, "Now that you have made an issue of it and have denied the statement of God's Word on this question, answer me this: Did you raise your boy right?"

He insisted that he did.

But I pressed the matter, "Did you ever have the family worship in your home?"

"No," he said. "We are busy people, working on the farm and I never had time for such things like some city people."

"Did you try to win your boy to Christ when he was small and when you had influence over him?" I asked.

"No," he said, "I never did believe in this business of begging little children into the church and overpersuading them."

I showed him what the Bible taught about it. "Suffer little children to come unto me and forbid them not." I showed him the command in the Bible, "And thou shalt teach them diligently unto thy children, and shalt talk of them when thou sittest in thine house, and when thou walkest by the way, and when thou liest down, and when thou risest up" (Deut. 6:7). Then I asked him, "Did you whip your boy and make him mind when he was a boy at home?"

He answered, "See here, Preacher, you cannot treat all children alike. My boy was a nervous, high-strung boy and he couldn't be punished like others could. It would just make him worse instead of better."

And then I honestly and faithfully told this father that he himself had sinned and that his boy was in the penitentiary because he had not followed the plain commands of God's Word about chastening his son and training him up in the way he should go.

Is Whipping Children Cruel?

Does it seem a cruel thing to whip a child? If you think so, then listen again to the Word of God:

"Withhold not correction from the child: for if thou beatest him with the rod, he shall not die. Thou shalt beat him with the rod, and shalt deliver his soul from hell."—Prov. 23:13, 14.

The doctor is not cruel who operates upon a sufferer to save his life. There may be some pain in the operation but the end to be attained is worth it all. The parent is not cruel who insists on long hours of study for the child in getting an education. The burden may be heavy, but the end attained is worth it. So the parent is not cruel who whips his child, severely if need be, frequently if necessary, persistently and reverently and prayerfully but determinedly, until he gets obedience and that meek and quiet spirit of reverence and obedience to authority.

Whip your children, readers, when they need it. They will not die; rather in old age they will rise up to call you blessed. "Thou shalt beat him with the rod, and shalt deliver his soul from hell."

Doubtless many are in Hell now because their parents never taught them that sin must be punished. They never did learn that "the wages of sin is death." They never did learn, "Be sure your sin will find you out." They never did learn from their parents, "Be not deceived, God is not mocked. For whatsoever a man soweth that shall he also reap." They never did learn that "the way of the transgressor is hard." They never did learn that turning to one's own way brings heartache and suffering and trouble and condemnation. Many, I say, are doubtless in Hell because they were not punished for sin as children.

Parents, as you love God and believe His Word, as you love your children and long for them to grow into good men and women, with the favor and blessing of God, then *demand obedience*, demand careful, quiet, immediate answers to questions, demand obedient action when you speak. Yes, teach your child that rebellion is as the sin of witchcraft and idolatry (I Sam. 15:23). By so teaching him now, you may have tears and heartache. You may be misunderstood. You may often despair and think you are failing. But one day, thank God, you will see the reward and will find that it pays to do what God has said. There is no way to have a happy home without discipline.

Do you know why many a mother is brought to shame by her children? Proverbs 29:15 tells us, "The rod and reproof give wisdom: but a child left to himself bringeth his mother to shame." Again Proverbs 29:17 says, "Correct thy son, and he shall give delight unto thy soul." Oh, the joy of well-brought-up young people, quiet, reverent, obedient, respectful! Such children are easy to win to Christ. They are easy to hold a job when they get one. They learn to study, learn to work, learn to avoid sin. God gives you some twenty years to make men and women out of your children. Be careful that you do not sin by avoiding punishment. Chastening is in God's plan of raising children! The home that does not have strict discipline is not a Bible kind of home. It will not have the peace of God long upon it.

The Boy Who Killed His Mother Was Never Spanked

On a certain March 5, the following appeared in the *Dallas Journal*:

> **DAD FORGIVES BOY WHO SLEW HIS MOTHER**
>
> CHICAGO, ILL., March 5 (UP).—Theodore Danielsen, who thought he had been bringing up a musical genius, decided today to forgive his son for killing his mother.
>
> Danielsen interviewed his 16-year-old son, Theodore, Jr., in jail last night. Teddy told him that he had killed his mother with a bread knife. Father and son wept together and the father listened to the boy's story, his arms around him, his head bowed.
>
> "I'm still your friend," the father said. "Keep your chin up. You're all I have left."
>
> To police, Danielsen said: "He has a very quick temper. We never spanked him."
>
> Teddy played the piano well and his teachers called him an "embryonic genius." Mrs. Danielsen, who also played the piano well, made him practice daily.
>
> Teddy killed her Thursday. She was making a cherry pie in the kitchen. He came in. She had learned that he hadn't been to school for two weeks. She reprimanded him and he picked up the bread knife off the table and ran it into her throat. He took $5 and her jewelry from his mother's purse and fled. Police arrested him yesterday.
>
> Teddy told police that he killed his mother because she slapped him and scratched his cheek and seemed about to slap him again. "HE HAS A VERY QUICK TEMPER. WE NEVER SPANKED HIM!"

That is the reason he had such a temper! The *Dallas Journal* then later comments editorially about this case that here is youth left free to express himself, without restraint.

Dear friend, happiness does not come to the home that has no authority, no discipline, no restraint, no punishment of sin. If you want the peace of God to abide in your home, then, Husband, Father, take your place as the minister of God, the head of the home and see that righteousness prevails there. It will take prayer, tears, pleading, and sometimes chastising. It will take good example and an earnest seeking after the right. But it is worth it, and there is no other way to have a home where God can abide in great blessing.

The Bible is never out of date, and in this matter it is as infallibly correct as it is on the plan of salvation. The home which is "the dearest place on earth, the nearest place to Heaven" is a home where there is peace and order, with a reverence and respect for authority which in the last analysis means a respect for God and a surrender to His will.

Christ Must Be Put First in the Home

Homes that are like Heaven must put Christ first. He was first in the creation. He it was who met Adam and talked with him in the Garden of Eden. God has planned that in Him all things should consist and that in all things He should have the pre-eminence. God has committed all judgment to the Son. Jesus Himself said, "All power in heaven and in earth is given unto me" (Matt. 28:18). So then, if you would have a happy and blessed home, put Christ first.

What part does the church have in your home? Is it counted an honor to be a church member? When you move your residence, do you immediately put your membership in a church of God's leading and choice, in the new community where you reside? And do you regularly attend the services whenever the doors are open? Are you in your place in Sunday school? in the morning and evening preaching services on Sunday? in the prayer meeting on Wednesday night? Do you take some active part, to fulfill your ministry, your stewardship of the Gospel? If not, how can you expect God to make such a home happy? Children will not follow the precept of a father and mother whose example does not tell the same thing.

It is a pitiful thing that it should even be necessary to say about parents, as Jesus said about the scribes and Pharisees, "Whatsoever they bid you observe, that observe and do; but do not ye after their works: for they say, and do not" (Matt. 23:3). Children will have no confidence in a hypocrite. They know whether you mean business for God. When they see you day by day putting business before the church, putting your pleasure before God, putting money-making before soul winning, reading other literature before the Bible, do you suppose they believe in the sincerity of your claims as a Christian? Do you suppose they are impressed by your devotion to God? Do you suppose they see any reason for trusting Christ and loving Him and serving Him? So, about many a parent it could honestly be said that, "What you do talks so loud I cannot hear what you say!" Put Christ first in your home if you want the peace of God to dwell there. We have it plainly said in the Word of God, "I the Lord thy God am a jealous God, visiting the iniquity of the fathers upon the children unto the third and fourth generation of them that hate me" (Exod. 20:5). You may expect your children to follow in your footsteps. You cannot expect them to love God and serve Him, to put Him first, unless you do the same.

At our home as a boy (it is one of my happy memories!) we always expected to go to church. My father, my step-mother, the whole family (too many to ride in one carriage!) went to church. We went when it was cold, we went when it was hot. We went when it rained, we went when it was dry. It was rare indeed that any were so sick they could not go, and if that were true, the rest of us went to church, and just one stayed at home to care for the sick. We went to church and Sunday school on time. We went to prayer meeting. I thank God for the happy memories that proved to me the sincerity of my father's faith in God.

Is Christ put first in your home? Do you have thanks at the table? Are little children taught to bow their heads and to be grateful to God for daily bread? Remember the disciples who in their sadness went down to Emmaus and were cheered with the presence of One whom they did not know. They recognized Him by the blessing of the bread! And your children can recognize Christ in you when they are accustomed to daily prayer, gratitude, to reverence in the home.

Does your home have Christian mottoes, Scripture verses on the walls? Are the children accustomed to hearing Mother and Father pray? Are they taught to lift their little voices in thanks and in petition? Are they accustomed to the Word of God as the fountain of blessing which Father and Mother have found it to be? I beg you, put Christ in your home if you want happiness there!

Recently I was in the home of a good man who had just died. He was a Christian. He said he was ready to go, and his family believed him. But they said to me, "Oh, Brother Rice, but we never heard him pray! If we could only have heard him pray!"

Home can only be a little bit of Heaven upon earth as Christ is recognized as the head of the home.

I am certain that even poverty and the attendant evils

and sorrows of it, are usually caused by our sins. The home where Christ is honored with the firstfruits of all the increase, is usually a prosperous and happy home. Every home should expect the blessing of Malachi 3:10, "Bring ye all the tithes into the storehouse, that there may be meat in mine house, and prove me now herewith, saith the Lord of hosts, if I will not open you the windows of heaven, and pour you out a blessing, that there shall not be room enough to receive it." Remember that Jesus Himself promised, "Give, and it shall be given unto you; good measure, pressed down, and shaken together, and running over, shall men give into your bosom" (Luke 6:38).

And where want, and poverty, and stark hunger is, it is likely true that those who have sowed sparingly have reaped sparingly. Where plenty is, even a modest plenty, with the blessing of God, it is often true that 'he that sowed bountifully, has reaped also bountifully' (II Cor. 9:6). Every home can claim the promise of Jesus: "Seek ye first the kingdom of God, and his righteousness; and all these things shall be added unto you." Daily food can come like manna from Heaven to those who trust Christ and put Him first and claim His promises.

Let every home, then, make God first in money matters and expect God's blessing in money matters.

Win Children to Christ

Blessed is the father who assumes the responsibility for the salvation of his children. Such fathers have come to me many times with great rejoicing to tell me when the last child has been converted. "Brother Rice, the last one is saved! We are all in the family of God and the circle will not be broken!"

The home cannot be happy where a prodigal boy or a

wayward girl breaks the hearts of Mother and Father. The home cannot be happy where the children grow up and forget Mother's God and Father's God. The only sure hope for happiness through the years is that as each child comes to the years of accountability, he be won to Christ, to love Him, to trust Him, to follow Him in baptism, to get in the church with God's people, to obey the Lord and grow in grace.

If you want the happiness in your home, win your children to Christ. In 1938, I wrote:

> Just a few months ago, God gave us our baby, Sarah Joy. The other five children had all been converted. We had rejoiced more than once that all of our little ones had now found peace in Christ and we would be a united family in Heaven. And now, with the joy that comes with our five-months-old baby, there comes also a heavy responsibility that we cannot shake off. I have just been thinking, Oh, what if we should all get to Heaven but this little one, and she be left outside!
>
> I have gotten accustomed now, with some difficulty, to speaking of "my six little girls" when I used to speak of "my five girls." Wouldn't it be a sad and terrible tragedy if, when we get to Heaven, Mrs. Rice and I would have to speak again of "our five little girls" and never mention the other, because we failed to win her to Christ?
>
> I thank God that He helped us with the other five. Each one, when they were five or six years old, were taught to trust in Christ, and did. With prayer, with tears, with deep anxiety, the other children were won to Christ.
>
> I will never forget how happy we were when the first one, Grace, found the Saviour. What a load lifted! Then Mary Lloys, the second girl, in 1930 while her mother was reading to her the story of the crucifixion from Matthew, suddenly burst into tears and said, "Mother! Mother, I want to be

saved!" And when little Joanna, the last one, found Christ, not long ago, we were so happy.

Now, what if the last one should be left outside! What if she should grow up without any faith in her father's God, without loving Christ or trusting Him? What if she should wander away and go in sin and break our hearts? Home could not be happy, as it ought to be, with one prodigal.

So, Father and Mother, I beg you, win your children to Christ.

Not long ago I was reading an old Bible given me by my father. I remember that he had given me to God to be a preacher when I was a baby. I never knew about it until long afterward, after my mother was dead. I learned that she had called me repeatedly, in letters to her loved ones, "My preacher boy." She had wanted me to preach the Gospel and begged God to make me a preacher. Then while reading in my father's Bible, I found underlined the words of Zacharias on the birth of his dear son, "His name is John." I thought, and my eyes filled with tears, that God had put it in the heart of my father that I might in some sense be a John the Baptist, a preacher in the spirit and power of Elijah, filled with the Holy Ghost, if not from my mother's womb, then at least throughout my ministry! And I wept and prayed that my father's prayers might be fulfilled and that in truth I might live up to my name!

Give your children to Christ.

Will I ever forget the day that my mother went home to Heaven! I was hardly six years old. We were called in from our play. Gathered around my mother's bed were my father and a number of kinspeople. All were weeping except my mother. She said to my cousin, "Georgia, won't you play and sing for me?" Cousin Georgia answered, "What shall I sing, Aunt Sadie?" My mother called for that old song which had blessed her heart so many times,

How firm a foundation, ye saints of the Lord
Is laid for your faith in His excellent Word.

So Cousin Georgia played it and tried to sing it, though she could not sing much for tears. Then my mother called us one by one and had us promise to meet her in Heaven. When we had promised, she looked up and said, "I can see Jesus and my baby now!" Then she smiled around at us and closed her eyes and went to sleep.

Oh, the joy in our home, because of the mother we had to win us to Christ! I was not saved then, but a little later I was converted, and the joy and peace of certainty of my heart on the matter of Christ and the Bible is largely guaranteed by the testimony of my sweet mother who is in Heaven!

"Christ Is the Head of This House"

In southwest Texas some years ago I went into a home hoping to win someone to Christ. There I found a newborn baby, three days old. The mother's heart was touched—it was her firstborn. I asked her if she wanted me to pray for the baby, and she gladly assented. I stooped over to put my hands upon the little red-faced fellow and to ask God to bless him, and then I thought, But what about the mother? So I asked her if I might pray for her, too. I said to her, "You will need the blessing of God to raise the little one. You will need power to lead him right. You need Christ. Are you not a Christian?" She answered that she was not, and she with some tears asked me to pray for her, too.

I turned to the father who, with pride over his son, sat nearby. "Are you a Christian?" I asked. He answered,

"No." I looked above the door, and there was a motto, *"Christ is the head of this house, the unseen guest at every meal, the silent listener to every conversation."* Then I asked him, "What is the meaning of this? That motto is not true. That is a lie on the walls of your home. You do not love Christ, you have not trusted Him. He is not the head of this home. Is that not so?"

The father dropped his head. He said, "Well, I know you are right. I guess I will have to take it down. No, Brother Rice, Christ is not the head of this house. I will take it down."

"I know something better than that," I said. "Why not just make it true today? Why not let Christ come in and be the head of this house? Let me pray for you while I pray for your baby. Let me pray that Christ will save you and make you a Christian?"

The Holy Spirit had brought conviction to his heart. He gave his consent, and with a deep concern all of us bowed our heads to pray. I placed my hands on the head of the little baby and prayed that God would help Mother and Father to raise the baby for Him, help them win the baby to Christ when he should reach the years of accountability. I prayed that their example would always lead him and bless him. I prayed then that the mother upon the bed with the baby on her arm should be saved, that she would fully trust Christ. I prayed that the father would give his whole heart to Christ, claim Him as Lord and Saviour. And they did trust Him, too. When the prayer was over, they took my hand and then and there dedicated their home to Christ. Christ came in to be the head of the house! I know it was a happy home.

Do you want a happy home like theirs? Then let Jesus Christ come in today to be the head of your house.

I thank God for a happy home. I thank Him for a wife who loves me and for children who are sweet and good. I thank God that all have trusted Christ as Saviour. I can truly say,

> **'Mid pleasures and palaces though we may roam,**
> **Be it ever so humble, there's no place like home;**
> **A charm from the skies seems to hallow us there,**
> **Which seek through the world, is ne'er**
> **met elsewhere.**
>
> **An exile from home splendor dazzles in vain;**
> **Oh, give me my lowly thatched cottage again;**
> **The birds singing gaily, that came at my call,**
> **Give me them, and that peace of mind dearer**
> **than all.**
>
> **Home, home sweet, sweet home.**
> **There's no place like home,**
> **Oh, there's no place like home.**

And many another like John Howard Payne, the writer, who never had a home of his own, could write these words, longing for the paradise and peace hereafter which here they have been denied.

If you have a home, guard it safely. Let Christ be there and have His way. But make sure of a home in Heaven.

One day we will gather in the heavenly home. Will the circle be unbroken? Are you ready to meet your mother, and your father, and all the loved ones gone on before? If not, then I beg you, get ready. Homes down here are frail things at best. We are troubled with all the sins and failures and mistakes that the flesh is heir to. The best home has been marred by sin. Even where every member of the family is a Christian, sin comes to bring misunderstandings and trouble. When death breaks the ties of home, we say good-by to Mother or Father at the grave. Distance ofttimes separates the chiefest loved ones. Children grow away from parents and leave. One grayheaded companion is left to mourn alone when the other is carried to the Silent City of the Dead. An earthly home at best is but a picture of a heavenly home when God Himself shall wipe away all tears from our eyes. One day Eden will be restored! One day we can meet our loved ones in the paradise of God!

Don't you want to meet Him in peace? Don't you want to be a part of the happy home there which God prepares for those who love Him?

Oh, think of the home over there
By the side of the river of life,
Of the saints all immortal and fair
In their home in the palace of light.

Today is a fleeting day. In the Father's house of many mansions we can have a home that will never be broken by death or sorrow. Whatever your lot here with its disappointments and failures, make sure that you have part in the home over there.

Jesus Christ is the way. Put your trust in Him today and have the peace and forgiveness and a bit of heaven in your heart! Then when He comes for His own, we will enter into the eternal rest and joy of Home, Sweet Home, with God!

4/ *God Blesses Big Families*

Do Not Be Deceived by the Propaganda of Socialists, Communists and the Ungodly About the "Population Explosion," About the Need to Limit Families. It Is Illogical and Unscriptural. God Blesses Big Families

"And God blessed them, and God said unto them, Be fruitful and multiply, and replenish the earth, and subdue it: and have dominion over the fish of the sea, and over the fowl of the air, and over every living thing that moveth upon the earth."—Gen. 1:28.

"And God blessed Noah and his sons, and said unto them, Be fruitful, and multiply, and replenish the earth."—Gen. 9:1.

"Lo, children are an heritage of the Lord: and the fruit of the womb is his reward. As arrows are in the hand of a mighty man; so are children of the youth. Happy is the man that hath his quiver full of them: they shall not be ashamed, but they shall speak with the enemies in the gate."—Ps. 127:3-5.

"Thy wife shall be as a fruitful vine by the sides of thine house: thy children like olive plants round about thy table. Behold, that thus shall the man be blessed that feareth the Lord."—Ps. 128:3, 4.

There is a great deal of foolish propaganda that Americans should limit their families, that the population is getting too great, too big for the earth to maintain, that the crowded conditions and the pollution of the air, the streams, the ocean, the land, make it necessary not to increase the population.

That propaganda is carried on largely as a fad by the ignorant but consciously, also, by socialist liberals and particularly by ungodly people. That position is unscriptural as we can clearly show. God blesses big families and encourages big families. And it would be good for America and good for the cause of Christ if God's people had big families and trained them well for Him.

I. THE BIBLE PLAINLY SAYS THAT MANY CHILDREN ARE A BLESSING

Consider the Scriptures above which give the Bible viewpoint, the Christian viewpoint, and the will of God for us concerning families.

1. The Command to Adam and Eve and to the Race Was to "Multiply, and Replenish the Earth"

If a man and wife have only two children, that is certainly not multiplying. In the long run, that is not even adding anything to the population. Only with a number of children could we properly use the term "multiply." That is the term God used.

He said the same thing to Noah in Genesis 9:1. Is not that command for the whole race?

2. Children Are a Special Gift From God

Psalm 127:3 says, "Lo, children are an heritage of the Lord: and the fruit of the womb is his reward." Every child is a blessing from God. God creates an immortal soul, and the husband and the wife are thus "heirs together of the grace of life" (I Pet. 3:7), are creators with God. And that is a wonderful heritage, a gift from God, a token of His loving care. In the very nature of the case, good Christians ought to expect that what God gives as a gift He will maintain and care for, if we love Him and rely on Him. The Scripture says, "The blessing of the Lord, it maketh rich, and he addeth no sorrow with it" (Prov. 10:22). And again Psalm 127:4 says that children are "as arrows. . .in the hand of a mighty man," more arrows and more armor for a strong man to defend himself. The more children, the more blessing and happiness and usefulness for a man. And so properly God says in the next verse, "Happy is the man that hath his quiver full of them." It is blessed for a man to have many children.

And the next Psalm tells of the great blessing of "every one that feareth the Lord; that walketh in his ways," for "thy wife shall be as a fruitful vine by the sides of thine house: thy children like olive plants round about thy table." A vine is expected to bear fruit every year. All sensible people think it proper that wild animals and domestic animals reproduce themselves regularly. Most of the mammals reproduce every year; smaller animals more often than that, and often with a litter of several puppies or cats or pigs, as the case may be. Obviously a fruitful wife would be like a fruitful vine, that is, the mother of a number of children, and "thy children like olive plants round about thy table" (Ps. 128:3). Again, the next verse says, "Behold, that thus shall the man be blessed that feareth the Lord." It is only by ignoring or contradicting these plain Scriptures that anyone could say that a large family among godly people is less than a great blessing.

3. Many Children Were Counted Normal and Blessed Fruitfulness, a Gift From God

In Deuteronomy 28 are many plain warnings to the people of Israel. If they would serve the Lord honestly and with all their hearts, He would give them great blessings. If not, then there would be a plague on their land, on their cattle, on their children, on their business, and on their nation. And Deuteronomy 28:62, 63 says, "Ye shall be left few in number, whereas ye were as the stars of heaven for multitude; because thou wouldest not obey the voice of the Lord thy God. And it shall come to pass, that as the Lord rejoiced over you to do you good, and to multiply you; so the Lord will rejoice over you to destroy you, and to bring you to nought; and ye shall be plucked from off the land whither thou goest to possess it."

Note that God counts it as a great blessing to be multiplied in number, to have many children. It is a curse of God to be fewer in number, with fewer children growing to adulthood.

But if the Jews would serve the Lord as they should, the "blessed shall be the fruit of thy body, and the fruit of thy ground, and the fruit of thy cattle, the increase of thy kine, and the flocks of thy sheep" (Deut. 28:4). Notice that children, "the fruit of thy body," are the first of the blessings numbered here in Deuteronomy 28:4. Normal fruitfulness is to have an increase of cattle, increase of flocks of sheep, increase of the fruits of the ground and normally, regular increase of children, "the fruit of thy body." Again in Deuteronomy 28:11 God says, "And the Lord shall make thee plenteous in goods, in the fruit of thy body, and in the fruit of thy cattle, and in the fruit of thy ground, in the land which the Lord sware unto thy fathers to give thee." Again, to be plenteous "in the fruit of thy body" is the first of the great blessings promised to those who serve the Lord. To have no children is a curse unspeakable, and to have few children is sad. And that is the normal impact of Scripture all the way through.

4. How Godly Women Longed and Prayed for Children!

One of the most moving stories in the Bible is that of Hannah, who was in bitterness of soul because she was barren and had no child, as told in I Samuel, chapter 1. In answer to earnest prayer God promised and gave her a son. He would be Samuel the great prophet, whom his mother lent unto the Lord as long as he should live. And you should delight to read Hannah's prophetic prayer of praise in I Samuel 2:1-11.

How often in the Bible did God give children in answer to beseeching prayer. So it was with Abraham and Sarah, even the promised Isaac when Abraham was a hundred years old and Sarah ninety!

We read in Genesis 25:21, "And Isaac intreated the Lord for his wife, because she was barren: and the Lord was intreated of him, and Rebekah his wife conceived." So the two children, Jacob and Esau, were born in answer to prayer. Read the pitiful prayers and concern of Rachel and Leah for children, each wanting more and each offering her maidservant to her husband that she might be counted the mother of more children, as you read in Genesis 30.

Remember how the wife of Manoah was barren, but an angel of the Lord came to tell the blessed news that Samson was to be born (Judges, chapter 13).

Remember the "great woman" of Shunem who made a prophet's chamber for Elisha in her home and how with great blessing he interceded with God so she could have a child (II Kings 4:8-17).

And from the first chapter of Luke we learn that John the Baptist was given, after long years of prayer, to Zacharias and Elisabeth. And the good news came, "Thy prayer is heard."

Only today in Old Jerusalem a man came to greet me who said, "I heard you years ago at Bob Jones University. You preached on John the Baptist who was given in answer to prayer and you asked all who wanted a son to pray then and there that God would give a son to be a preacher, a prophet of God, and eight or nine couples stood pledging themselves to such a prayer. "And," said this friend who was present, "I think everyone of those couples had a son born in answer to prayer." Yes, and I remember one couple who had been married fourteen years and had longed for a child and that day they claimed God's promise and within about a year a son was born and is being trained to preach the Gospel.

Now, only one who is spiritually blind would surely fail to see that by Bible standards it is blessed to have many children. "Children are an heritage of the Lord" and they are "as arrows. . .in the hand of a mighty man," and blessed "is the man that hath his quiver full of them."

5. How Much Blessing the World Would Have Missed Had Mothers of Great Men Had Fewer Children!

A thousand examples could be given to show that, with godly parents, many children are a great blessing. One famous example is John Wesley who was the thirteenth of nineteen children born to Susannah Wesley and her husband James. And Charles, the sweet singer and song writer, was the seventeenth child. How poor would have been the world had Susannah Wesley only had two or three children!

Dr. Bob Jones, Sr., was the eleventh child. Oh, the thousands of souls who would have gone to Hell unwarned and unconverted had God not given that great evangelist to a godly, praying mother, the eleventh child!

Benjamin Franklin's father had thirteen children. Benjamin was the last of the boys.

My father had eight children who grew to adulthood besides some babies who died in infancy. I was the fourth child. If my father had had only two or three children, God would not have given me in answer to my mother's and father's prayer that He give them a preacher. My brother, Dr. Bill Rice, greatly used evangelist and head of probably the largest missionary work to the deaf people in the world, was number eight. Would my father have served God and his country better had my brother Bill never been born? Do you suppose that when godly parents bring a child into the world it is a curse to the world? Is it wicked, unthinking unbelief? For godly parents who bring children into the world to be taught and saved and made into godly Christians and good citizens, every child born is a great blessing of God to the world. Those who speak for smaller families make evil good and good evil and teach men not to obey the plain command of God to multiply and replenish the earth.

II. MARRIAGE IS INTENDED TO PRODUCE CHILDREN AND BE FRUITFUL

The idea of marriage has been greatly debased in the popular mind. In America about one-third of all marriages end in divorce. Sex is so exploited and promoted in movies, in literature, in advertising, in nudity, in open immorality, that it is not seen as holy and proper normal love between a husband and wife which God had planned for families. Since sexual indulgence is promoted and encouraged outside of marriage, and marriage itself has lost its sanctity in the minds of many, the natural result is that the blessedness of children has been lost sight of in the popular mind. The more people turn back to love for the Bible and faith in God and the moral standards of the Bible, then much more people have the proper attitude about families and the blessing of many children.

1. God Made Men and Women With the Sex Urge That Would Normally Lead to the Frequent Conception and Birth of Children

It is true that the sex act in marriage is a matter of love and communion and pleasure. Certainly the Lord did not mean that the mating of husband and wife should be only for procreation.

However, it is still true that in all God's animal world the sex act is intended and expected to propagate the species. God certainly permits the sex acts in the context of a husband and wife, in proper marriage, to be a pleasure, but it is still obviously true that primarily the sex act is intended to procreate, just as the sex act is so intended in the animal world. Animals may mate for pleasure or by instinct, but God intended it to reproduce, and certainly that must have been God's intention with mankind.

And not only so, but God encourages the unlimited and unrestricted mating of husband and wife. He says, "Marriage is honourable in all, and the bed undefiled" (Heb. 13:4). He places no restrictions on the normal married life of husband and wife. And there is not ever a hint in the Bible that a husband and wife should restrain and limit themselves so as not to beget children. Rather, the Lord insists in I Corinthians 7:1-6 that neither the husband nor the wife defraud the other, that each should seek to satisfy the desires, needs and happiness of the mate. If they feel they should, they are permitted to stay apart for a little time for fasting and prayer, but this is permitted and not commanded. It seems to be the intent of God in making men and women as He did and establishing the institution of marriage as He has, and encouraging perfect freedom of husbands and wives with each other in the normal enjoyment of married love, that God Himself would decide when to give children, and probably He would give them frequently through the childbearing life of the wife. There is nothing in the Bible to indicate that God ever intended a husband and wife to limit the number of children they would have.

2. In One Case God Killed a Man for Refusing to Have Children

In Genesis 38:6-10 we read:

"And Judah took a wife for Er his firstborn, whose name was Tamar. And Er, Judah's firstborn, was wicked in the sight of the Lord; and the Lord slew him. And Judah said unto Onan, Go in unto thy brother's wife, and marry her, and raise up seed to thy brother. And Onan knew that the seed should not be his; and it came to pass, when he went in unto his brother's wife, that he spilled it on the ground, lest that he should give seed to his brother. And the thing which he did displeased the Lord: wherefore he slew him also."

Onan was commanded to "go in unto thy brother's wife, and marry her, and raise up seed to thy brother." He did not do it, and while it was his father who had commanded him, it evidently was the will of God also. And when Onan intentionally prevented conception, God killed him!

The Scriptures nowhere expressly forbids "planned parenthood" and birth control. I do not suppose it would be a sin if a man and wife wanted six children but hoped not to have ten or twelve. I think they would probably be mistaken if they set out to limit what God in loving mercy would give them, but the Bible nowhere clearly states that it is wrong to limit families.

But it is obviously counted a sin for a man not to want children as a result of marriage. Families that do not want any children certainly are wrong, and I would infer from this Scripture that those who do not intend to have a considerable family are thus intending to cheat God's plan, and they displease Him.

3. The Experience of the Race, the Testimony of Millions, Is That Normally Large Families Are Blessed of God

This idea that one or two or three children are greatly to be preferred to four or five or six is the idea of a scant minority, not generally the conclusion of those who have big families. Susannah Wesley, mother of John and Charles and seventeen more, never lamented the fact that God gave her too many children. Everyone was taught to obey, was raised to be happy and useful and cooperative. In our home of six daughters, five came along, we think by God's planning, about two or three years apart. Then there was a six-year wait before our last baby came. We named her Sarah Joy—Sarah for my mother and Joy because she was so much desired, so greatly loved, and such a happy blessing. Mrs. Rice and I had frankly thought we might have ten, but God planned it otherwise and we are content.

You may think that a mother in a poor family, with ten children and a small home, greatly regrets that she has so many. If you think that, you have never worked much among poor people. It is true that sometimes the drinking, cigarette-smoking kind of mother who wants a night life, who never disciplines the children, never prays with them, does not enjoy her children. Sometimes undisciplined children turn out to be brats that nobody wants around. That is not because there were too many children. Even one of that kind of a spoiled, undisciplined, self-willed child would be undesirable. But the mothers and the fathers of many children take great joy in their large families.

What a happy time we had around the table at mealtime! What games we had in the home! How many others crowded in to see us! What fellowship when singing around the piano! I feel sorry for the boy who never has a sister or a younger brother, or the girl who never has other sisters with whom she may share, and brothers of whom she can be proud. The truth is that with all the propaganda of the Planned Parenthood Association, and the Women's Lib Movement, and the promotion of the left-wing press and in women's magazines, the great multitude of poor women who have many children do not go to the clinics to get birth control devices, do not bother about the rhythm method of controlling conception, and do not seek to limit their children. It is a simple fact, obvious to those who take time to check into the matter, that those who have children who are well reared and disciplined and godly, are in nearly every case happy with a big family. The testimony of the race is that God's plan is a good plan, that big families are blessed of God.

Would you think that large families moan the fact that they cannot send all the children to college? That was not true in my father's home with his eight children. Three of us went on to college and to graduate school. Three others did some college and Bible school work. Sure, we worked our way through college, and all of us have always felt that it was a great blessing that we had a big family and we were proud of each other and of our name.

Mrs. Rice and I have six daughters. Since 1926 we have had no regular salary, no regular agreement about income with anybody but the Lord. Naturally we have been very poor some of the time. I mean that we had a second-hand, Model-T Ford car, that we had no kitchen cabinet for years, and that we lived modestly and carefully, on a relatively small income. And yet all six of my daughters have AB degrees, two of them have masters degrees from college, three of them have books published, two are college teachers; all six are married to full-time Christian workers. Of course, besides helping with the work at home, they helped at typing, helped at mailing out THE SWORD OF THE LORD, worked long hours at office work to help buy their clothes and help pay their way through college. Was that bad? None of them think so. And everyone of them would rather have their sisters than to have had any more luxuries. Not a one of the girls had a car of her own, none took vacations in Florida or to the ski resorts, yet they made top grades in college and were counted most gifted and desirable young women. What did they lose by having eight in the family?

The simple truth is that in loving mercy God takes care of what He gives. When He gives a baby, those who trust Him will find that He will take care of the baby. God makes a way for those who have good families and enjoy them and rear them in godliness and for God. A big family, and poor? Yes, but not a spoiled brat among them, not a drop-out, not a dope user, not a cigarette smoker, not a divorcee, not a problem child among them. The experience of millions of happy families proves that the "do-gooders," the calamity-howlers about the "population explosion," are wrong when they say that families can take care of their children better and train them better and make them happier with fewer children. It simply is not true.

III. SOLID ANSWERS TO THE FOOLISH AND WICKED EXCUSES FOR AVOIDING GOOD FAMILIES

Let us concede that in India, in Ceylon, in China, and in some other benighted countries, there is some problem about having and raising food enough for everybody. But closer examination indicates that there are other overriding problems which are not essentially a population problem.

Suppose a man in India works a little plot of ground with one water buffalo, plants his rice by hand (a poor quality of seed), reaps it with a small hand sickle, thrashes it by beating out the grain by hand and winnowing it in the wind—suppose such a man has trouble raising enough rice for his family and buying other necessities of life. But good, scientific farmers have found that by selecting a superior strain of rice, and cultivating it carefully even by hand, one can make twice as much rice on the same land with the same work and have more than enough rice for his family needs and to buy other necessities. And then if a few modern and ordinary pieces of equipment can be introduced and men taught to use them, the same man can take care of three times as much ground and raise eight or ten times as much food as he has been accustomed to doing. His problem was not a population explosion; it was a problem of ignorance, tradition, illiteracy, and also probably partly a problem of heathen religion.

India has trouble raising enough food for its immense population. Yet cattle roam the streets and block traffic, while people sleep in the streets at night, and some of them die on the streets, and these same cattle, unused, undisciplined, walk over them or around them. Yet, with an abundance of beef cattle they go hungry because it is against their religious superstition to eat meat.

Monkeys and baboons waste millions of dollars worth of food. But it would be counted a sin to strike a monkey with a stick because he may be the reincarnated ancestor, come back to live again in the monkey. The problem there is a foolish waste, careless management and hindrances of superstition and false religion and tradition. There is still enough work to be done in the world to keep everybody busy if everybody would work at it. And honest work can earn enough food and clothing and necessary comforts.

Because there is a multitude of women, usually black women, with large families of illegitimate children, on relief and taking sometimes $40 a month per child from the welfare chest, naturally people feel that such women have too many children. Well, any illegitimate child born out of marriage is too many. I would have no special objection on insisting that any woman be sterilized after she has her second illegitimate child, if she wants to be on relief. I think it would not be a sin to stop the multiplication of the big, big flood of illegitimate children without a responsible father and, of course, not a family at all in the real sense. That is no argument against legitimate families of the Bible pattern, godly people, raising decent, respectable, hard-working, godly children.

I say, there are good, solid answers to those who suggest that people should be taxed for every extra child or be given a premium for not having children and otherwise insisting that families be kept down to two or three children at the most.

1. "But a Father and Mother Cannot Adequately Take Care of a Big Family"

So some say. But millions of families have found that the clothes of the oldest child can be handed down to the second one. Older girls can take care of the new baby. Where there are several girls there is no hardship but proper training and usefulness and happiness when they learn to cook, to wash, to care for babies, to clean the house, to help

Mother; and it is silly to suppose that they cannot do that and go to school and make good grades, as thousands of families have proved again and again. And if a big family is hard for one man to support, then the older boys or older girls help out. The simple truth is that a very large proportion of married women now want to work anyhow, and it is far better for people to learn to work and help provide for the family while they are young and without family responsibilities.

I am thinking of a very poor family in depression times. The father could do only manual labor, and he never made much money. Two boys carried paper routes, one boy worked in a store, another boy sold papers on the streets, Mama took in some washings and daughter helped her. Some years went by and I went back to the church where that family attended. The younger son who had sold papers on the street drove up in a Cadillac car; he was chairman of the board of deacons and president of his company. The big family did not suffer loss by being big.

2. "But College Expenses Are So Heavy and I Want All My Children to Go to College"

Well, all your children ought not go to college, unless they are unusual. I think that half the people who attend college now do not much want to go to college. They go as a matter of prestige and because of the pride of Dad and Mother. In many, many cases a third of the freshman class and sometimes half, either drop out or fail the first year. Girls go to college with little aim but a good time and to meet the man they hope to marry. Many a boy would do better to take a good high school course, perhaps in a technical high school, and get into some business or job that his heart would be in and where he could make good and be prosperous and useful. Many a girl would be better to marry her high school sweetheart, learn to work to help make a living, learn to save, to use money wisely, and without the expensive tastes generated by four wild years in college so that she could not be happy and probably not be successful as the wife of a poor man.

But some should go to college. Anybody who ought to go to college in America can go to college. There are scholarships that go begging, and people who are willing to work can earn their way without a scholarship. Literally thousands of young men and women are doing it. They are the serious kind. They are fit for college and college can do them good. In nearly every case there are ways to borrow money to help on college expenses, and in nearly every case a family with eight children can see nearly all of them, or all of them, go to college just as easily as a family with two children can get those two through college. And they will be better adjusted to society and better ready for solid, good careers afterward, and for happy marriages.

3. "But the Population Is About to Be More Than the World Can Feed, and There Won't Be Enough Food for the Millions Who Will Be Here in a Few Years"

Again, that is a silly statement. Right now all over America farmers have to have a quota. They are not allowed to raise more than a certain amount of food. One farmer in Michigan suffered the loss of his farm. The government took it away from him because he planted more wheat than the farm authorities thought he should. He wanted that wheat to feed his chickens and was doing a big business. But the left-wingers in the government wanted him to buy his feed from other farmers. There was too much wheat being raised anyhow! So the government wickedly took the man's farm away from him and he moved to Australia.

There is such a big production of foodstuffs that farmers constantly complain that they have trouble getting high enough prices to pay their expenses. Stockmen constantly bring pressure on the government to forbid the importation of beef from Argentina or Australia. In America we can raise more meat, can raise more wheat, can raise more vegetables than we can possibly consume.

I grew up in West Texas. At the age of ten I was on a ranch of six thousand acres. Farmers moved into that area and I saw the ranch cut up into perhaps twenty farms. However, I went back there later and found most of that land has been turned back into grazing land. It is not needed to produce foodstuffs now and that makes it "marginal land." It could be used again for farming if it were needed. But it is not.

Farming is often inefficient on small farms. Some farms may raise 30 bushels of corn to an acre, some other farmers raise 200 bushels to the acre! And constantly the number of people on farms is decreasing because with modern machinery one man can feed a multitude with farm products.

And there is much fuel left in the world. There is still an abundance of coal, but since gas is often cheaper and less trouble, some mines closed down. The union of miners has raised wages until some mines are not profitable. There are still millions of tons of coal in America. The oil industry is carefully policed to keep from exploiting too quickly the great reserves which are being found. The greatest oil deposits this world has have recently been discovered up in northern Alaska and Canada but have not been opened yet.

There are mineral resources not yet discovered or explored. It is a foolish argument against having normal families because busybodies complain that some day there will not be enough food or material to supply the needs of all.

4. "But Increasing Population Means Increased Pollution of the Air, the Land, the Oceans Until the Earth Will Become Uninhabitable"

Now there are pollution problems, but there are not necessary population problems. When the population was very thin, when we had no plumbing but outdoor privys, flies were everywhere and typhoid fever was common and often deadly. The answer to the problem was not fewer people, but more sanitary measures.

When open sewers ran down the streets, as they once did, they were health hazards. They smelled badly, they caused extra trouble. That problem was a pollution problem but not a population problem. Many a small village or town has had a dump where every kind of refuse was dumped. It was an eyesore and it was taking up land that could be used for cultivation. But as the city got larger, people made more definite plans to take care of garbage and waste. But that is a poor argument to bring against godly people having normal, large, healthy families, well-reared and godly, as the Bible commands. The well-reared children of godly parents will not throw empty beer cans by the roadside nor litter the beaches with garbage nor pollute the air with cigarette smoke.

About the worst thing that could happen for America would be for Christian people, the educated people, the well-disciplined, moral people to stop raising good families and let the world be overrun by the ignorant, the illiterate, the immoral, the illegitimate and the lazy. Every Christian home that raises good families and teaches them the Bible and gets the children saved and makes good, loyal, patriotic citizens and teaches them to make an honest living, is contributing to the health and welfare of America, not only in spiritual values but in every value dear to good people.

We should also consider that the propaganda for "planned family" limitations and birth control comes very largely from groups that are not well capable of moral judgment and are not to be trusted in leadership. Official "planned parenthood" clinics and the women's liberation movement and socialists and communists who want godly people to limit their families, and the wild-eyed youngsters in college, irresponsible, smoking pot, taking over college buildings, assaulting or insulting police, burning draft cards, couples living in sin without marriage—all these would like to pass rules for smaller families. Girls living like harlots want free abortion clinics. They want all the laws repealed that would punish drug using. They want the wild rock-'n'-roll festivals. They are against all the traditional standards and values that made America great. They are not to be trusted for moral leadership and to make moral judgments. Yet those are the kinds of people who do the principal argument about limiting families and pushing birth control, advocating sterilization after one or two babies, advocating extra taxes for extra children. That advice is silly, irresponsible, illogical and anti-scriptural.

So, Christians, thank God for fine, big families. Have them, enjoy them, love them, train them, discipline them, win them to Christ, make of them great Christian workers and citizens.

5/ *Beautiful Women in Public and Private*

"Whose adorning let it not be that outward adorning of plaiting the hair, and of wearing of gold, or of putting on of apparel; But let it be the hidden man of the heart, in that which is not corruptible, even the ornament of a meek and quiet spirit, which is in the sight of God of great price."—I Pet. 3:3,4.

"In like manner also, that women adorn themselves in modest apparel, with shamefacedness and sobriety; not with broided hair, or gold, or pearls, or costly array; But (which becometh women professing godliness) with good works."—I Tim. 2:9, 10.

Here are two passages of Scripture concerning a woman's adornment. You will notice that the first passage quoted above has reference to a woman and her husband. And it tells how a woman can be beautiful and attractive to her husband.

The second passage relates to a woman's appearance in public and her work in the church, as the context shows us.

In both cases the Scriptures emphasize that true beauty in a woman is in her character, and in each case it plays down those things stressed by the world—elaborate hairdos, jewels, costly clothes and the effort to reveal the woman's figure in order to attract men.

"Wasn't the bride beautiful?" they say after every wedding. And there is a sense in which every good woman, who loves and is loved, is beautiful. God intended it so. God made woman as a helper, meet for the man and surely to add to his comfort, his pleasure and joy. If God made men to love the beautiful, surely He intended women to be attractive and beautiful.

However, God's idea of beauty and the world's idea are different. And Christian women should learn what God has to say on this matter.

The breaking down of the home on every side of us, the increase in adultery, in rape, the great incidence of venereal disease, and the shameless nudity and near-nudity means that good women, unless they would sin grievously, must find what God says about the adorning and true beauty of women, to have beauty with character, with modesty, with purity; to earn and have the permanent respect and love and companionship of husbands and to be revered and trusted and obeyed by their children.

And you may be sure that the short shorts, the bikini bathing suits, the stretch pants that are intended to reveal a woman's every shape, the miniskirts calculated to stir men by showing women's thighs, the hot pants, and the scantiness of the clothes intended to show much of a woman's body and make her sexually attractive to all the onlookers—surely that shows that good women should learn what God commands about "modest apparel."

Let us notice in passing that I Peter 3:3 puts "wearing of gold, or of putting on of apparel" in the same sentence. God does not forbid the wearing of apparel, so He does not forbid plaiting of the hair and wearing of gold. But they are played down here; they are not a woman's chief adornment.

How wise and how beautiful is the woman who learns God's beauty, to win and make happy and to hold the love of her husband; and God's beauty in character, to make her Christian influence what it ought to be.

I. WOMEN ARE TO BE BEAUTIFUL TO THEIR HUSBANDS BY LOVING OBEDIENCE

The passage in I Peter 3, verses 3 and 4, is in the midst of a longer passage and we need to observe the context:

"Likewise, ye wives, be in subjection to your own husbands; that, if any obey not the word, they also may without the word be won by the conversation of the wives; While they behold your chaste conversation coupled with fear. Whose adorning let it not be that outward adorning of plaiting the hair, and of wearing of gold, or of putting on of apparel; But let it be the hidden man of the heart, in that which is not corruptible, even the ornament of a meek and quiet spirit, which is in the sight of God of great price. For after this manner in the old time the holy women also, who trusted in God, adorned themselves, being in subjection unto their own husbands: Even as Sara obeyed Abraham, calling him lord: whose daughters ye are, as long as ye do well, and are not afraid with any amazement. Likewise, ye husbands, dwell with them according to knowledge, giving honour unto the wife, as unto the weaker vessel, and as being heirs together of the grace of life; that your prayers be not hindered."—I Pet. 3:1-7.

It is obvious here that God speaks of a woman's relation to her husband. In the preceding chapter, verses 13 and 14 tell us that Christians are to "submit yourselves to every ordinance of man for the Lord's sake; whether it be to the king, as supreme; Or unto governors, as unto them that are sent by him for the punishment of evildoers, and for the praise of them that do well." And we are told in verse 18 of that preceding chapter, "Servants, be subject to your masters with all fear; not only to the good and gentle, but also to the froward." And with that background, the inspired apostle writes, "Likewise, ye wives, be in subjection to your own husbands. . . ."

As citizens are to obey the rulers and as servants are to obey their masters, so wives are to obey their husbands.

1. Thus Win an Unsaved Husband

And here is a wonderfully sweet promise: "That, if any obey not the word, they also may without the word be won by the conversation of the wives; While they behold your chaste conversation coupled with fear." The word *conversation* here originally meant *manner of life*. So the unsaved husband who will not obey the Word of God as preached by the preacher, can be won by the loving, obedient wife, as the husband observes her manner of life. Because, in truth, nothing is a better index of real Christian character in a woman than the fact that she keeps her marriage vow to love and honor and obey her husband until death should part them.

In some sense, a married woman's first duty is to be a good wife. And while that may take time and a woman may prefer some quicker, easier way, God's way often is that a lost husband will not be won unless his wife proves to be a good Christian by loving and obeying him, as she promised to do.

Perhaps someone says, "But that will not work! I believe that a lost husband simply would lead the wife into further sin to dishonor God!"

My answer simply is this: I did not write this Scripture;

God had it written in the Bible. And if you do not believe this part of the Bible will work, why believe any part of the Bible will work? Do you want to get your scissors and cut out just the parts of the Bible you do not believe, as a modernist or an infidel would? No, here is God's plan.

In Ephesians 5:22 wives are commanded, ". . . submit yourselves unto your own husbands, as unto the Lord," that is, as if it were the Lord to whom she submits! And then Ephesians 5:24, two verses later, says, "Therefore as the church is subject unto Christ, so let the wives be to their own husbands in every thing." Note those words "IN EVERY THING."

And now in I Peter 3, the Lord simply commands that a wife is to obey even an unsaved husband and thus by doing so, to win him.

The command for a wife to obey her husband is much clearer and stronger in the Bible than any command to attend church or sing in the choir.

Many a Christian woman has tried her best to impress her husband by bobbing her hair, by eye shadow and mascara and lipstick and perfume and fashionable clothes, but found that does not hold a man's respect or a man's love. So the wise woman here will listen to what God says:

"Whose adorning let it not be that outward adorning of plaiting the hair, and of wearing of gold, or of putting on of apparel; But let it be the hidden man of the heart, in that which is not corruptible, even the ornament of a meek and quiet spirit, which is in the sight of God of great price."

You remember that Jesus said, "Blessed are the meek: for they shall inherit the earth" (Matt. 5:5). Then meekness of heart of a woman toward her husband is the way for her to inherit the kind of love and respect and fellowship which a man wants to give to his wife and which is a part of true married happiness.

Every man needs someone who loves him, right or wrong; loves him so much that he is really first among all human beings. Every man needs somebody to whom he can say, "I am first with this one. She loves me and trusts me and wants me and would do anything possible to make me happy." One of the five great blessings named in Psalm 103:1-5 is that God "crowneth thee with lovingkindness and tender mercies." When a man has a wife whose loving-kindness and tenderness and admiration toward him makes him really a king among men, happy is he!

And any man has a right to feel cheated and defrauded when he marries a wife, sets out to support her, gives her his name, saves himself for her, then finds that she lied and cheated in her marriage vows and perjures her soul day by day with rebellion when she promised obedience, thus she is a wife by law and by the ceremony, but she does not play a wife's part and is not in her own heart's devotion a wife.

Oh, what beauty there is to the husband in a woman who truly loves him, submits to him, longs to please him, and lives to make him happy! Here is the wife's true beauty to her husband.

2. The Lovely Example of Sarah

The Bible says to good women, "Here is the example that proves what is good." The Scripture says,

"For after this manner in the old time the holy women also, who trusted in God, adorned themselves, being in subjection unto their own husbands: Even as Sara obeyed Abraham, calling him lord: whose daughters ye are, as

long as ye do well, and are not afraid with any amazement."

Do you know why our mothers or perhaps, better, our grandmothers, had long life and held the constant love and affection of their husbands? Do you know why such families held together through thick and thin, through poverty or wealth, through dark hours and bright? And the children rose up to call the mother blessed? Why those good women, like my mother, who never went to a beauty parlor, who washed the family clothes over a rub board and boiled them in a big iron pot in the yard and these grandmothers who churned their own butter, who ground their own sausage, cured their own pork, made their own lye soap, made all their clothes and those of the children, and the shirts and underwear for her men—those women who bore many children, and had homemade rag carpets on the floor, yet held the steadfast devotion and respect and love of their husbands and children.

In my boyhood I do not remember but one divorce among all the people we knew about, and a "grass widow" was in disgrace.

So "Sara obeyed Abraham, calling him lord." Godly women today should be daughters to Sarah and likewise love and respect and honor their husbands, making them happy by their meek and quiet spirit here commanded, and being in subjection which they promised and vowed before God and men to do.

Did you notice the Scripture says that this beauty, this adorning, which God recommends, is "of the heart, in that which is not corruptible"? Oh, a woman who depends on a beautiful form and on hairdo and cosmetics and jewelry and fashion to keep her beautiful, cannot escape the ravages which age brings. The woman of thirty does not have the bright freshness and charm of the girl of eighteen or twenty perhaps. Before long her breasts sag, she gets heavy in the abdomen and hips. There are lines around the eyes and a droop to the corners of her mouth, and streaks of gray in the hair. Oh, human beauty corrupts so soon.

But it is remarkable that Sarah's beauty seemed never to grow old to Abraham and to others about her! After Sarah was about ninety years old and before the birth of Isaac, Abraham in Gerar was greatly distressed lest the man of the place should kill him in order to get beautiful Sarah! (Gen. 20). Oh, he thought she was beautiful!

You see, a smile is still beautiful whether it is from one sixteen or sixty. And loving attention, tender ministrations, sympathetic understanding and glad surrender to the good husband she loves are beauties that are not corruptible! These are the ornaments which a godly woman ought to show to her husband, "Even as Sara obeyed Abraham, calling him lord. . . ."

3. God Commands a Woman to Have Long Hair As a Token of Her Subjection to Her Father or Husband

In I Corinthians 11 is a teaching which timid preachers often leave out. But there God explains:

"But I would have you know, that the head of every man is Christ; and the head of the woman is the man; and the head of Christ is God."

Therefore, when a man prays he should uncover his head as a sign that there is no pope nor bishop to stand between him and Christ. That is why good men take off their hats in church and when they pray, and why men do not wear long hair.

"But every woman that prayeth or prophesieth with her head uncovered dishonoureth her head: for that is even all one as if she were shaven. For if the woman be not covered, let her also be shorn: but if it be a shame for a woman to be shorn or shaven, let her be covered. For a man indeed ought not to cover his head, forasmuch as he is the image and glory of God: but the woman is the glory of the man. For the man is not of the woman; but the woman of the man. Neither was the man created for the woman; but the woman for the man. For this cause ought the woman to have power on her head because of the angels. Nevertheless neither is the man without the woman, neither the woman without the man, in the Lord. For as the woman is of the man, even so is the man also by the woman; but all things of God. Judge in yourselves: is it comely that a woman pray unto God uncovered? Doth not even nature itself teach you, that, if a man have long hair, it is a shame unto him? But if a woman have long hair, it is a glory to her: for her hair is given her for a covering."—I Cor. 11:5-15.

Note the teaching here. A woman's long hair is given as a glory to her for it is given her for a covering (vs. 15). But if a man has long hair, it is a shame to him because it would indicate submission in a sense that is not required of men and would be denying the responsibility which God puts on a man to lead his family for God.

And so because of the angels who look on, when a woman prays she ought to have the veiling or covering of long hair as a sign of her submission. Does this mean that the holy angels would be shocked at this sign of disobedience perhaps? Or it seems likely even that the one sin an angel might be tempted mostly to commit would be rebellion? That was the sin of the archangel Lucifer when he fell and became Satan. That was the sin of the angels who fell with him. And, oh, how shameful for a woman not to live a life of obedience to her husband which she vowed before God and men to do. Surely, then, it is shameful for a woman not to have a token of that obedience on her head.

I go into this in more detail in the book, *Bobbed Hair, Bossy Wives and Women Preachers*. But there is no use for anybody to say that this part of the Bible is now out of date or that, although God commands it, it is not important. Woman's hair is a part of her beauty and her glory, and so it is connected with that modesty and obedience and subjection to father or husband which God requires of a good woman.

Some people think that a hat worn in church, or a lace cap, fills this requirement. I think they misunderstand the Scripture and miss the point where God says, "For her hair is given her for a covering," that is, literally "a veiling" in verse 15 above.

A devout man of another denomination came to Dr. Jack Hyles in Hammond, Indiana, wishing to go with him from house to house and learn how to do personal soul winning. But he was dressed in the traditional clerical garb of a collar turned around backwards, making him look like a Roman priest. Dr. Hyles said, "I will be glad to have you go with me soul winning, but you would be misunderstood with that garb. If you will change into a business suit so you will not mislead people, then you can go with me to win souls."

But his wife interrupted boldly and said, "He will do nothing of the sort! He will not take off his minister's garb!"

Dr. Hyles said, "What is the meaning of that little lace cap you wear?"

She replied, "It is a sign of my submission to my husband."

Dr. Hyles replied, "I would rather have the submission than the lace cap."

Oh, Christian women, what treasure is that adornment of a meek and quiet spirit which in the sight of God is of great price!

II. WOMEN ARE TO BE ADORNED IN PUBLIC BY MODEST APPAREL, MODEST FACE AND GOOD WORKS

The passage in I Peter, chapter 3, obviously relates to a wife and her husband. But the passage in I Timothy 2:9 and 10 relates specifically to a Christian woman in relation to the church and the public. So we need to read the entire context.

"In like manner also, that women adorn themselves in modest apparel, with shamefacedness and sobriety; not with broided hair, or gold, or pearls, or costly array; But (which becometh women professing godliness) with good works. Let the woman learn in silence with all subjection. But I suffer not a woman to teach, nor to usurp authority over the man, but to be in silence. For Adam was first formed, then Eve. And Adam was not deceived, but the woman being deceived was in the transgression. Notwithstanding she shall be saved in childbearing, if they continue in faith and charity and holiness with sobriety."—I Tim. 2:9-15.

1. The Woman Should Adorn Herself With Meekness in Public

Here we are told, "Let the woman learn in silence with all subjection." Sometimes in a service God's men take turns speaking to the people. The woman is not to do that but is to learn in silence, and Paul was inspired to say, "But I suffer not a woman to teach, nor to usurp authority over the man, but to be in silence." So in Bible times there were no women preachers, no women teachers of men.

We are reminded that the woman was made after the man and for the man, and that in the case where Adam listened to his wife, he was led into sin and the ruin of the fall. Yet God has a place for women and "notwithstanding she shall be saved in childbearing, if they continue in faith and charity and holiness with sobriety." The glory of a good woman is to be in her husband and children, not in public leadership or authority over men or young men.

We need not here go into detail, but it is clear from the Scriptures that a woman may teach other women and may teach children (Titus 2:3-5). So widows are to be honored "if she have brought up children" (I Tim. 5:10). It seems clear that Timothy was taught in the faith by his mother and grandmother (I Tim. 1:5). And Priscilla, working with her husband Aquila, took Apollos home with them "and expounded unto him the way of God more perfectly" (Acts 18:26). The mother of Jesus and other women were in that pentecostal prayer meeting (Acts 1:14).

So a woman is to take a woman's place in the Lord's work, a place of subjection to other leaders in the church as she is in subjection to her husband at home. And this should not be any trial for a good woman, because all the other Christians, too, are commanded, "Obey them that have the rule over you, and submit yourselves: for they watch for your souls, as they that must give account, that they may do it with joy, and not with grief: for that is unprofitable for you" (Heb. 13:17).

And no doubt a woman's appearance and apparel and attitude should be influenced by this fact that she is man's helper in the home or in the church, not his leader or boss.

2. The Christian Woman Should Have "Modest Apparel, With Shamefacedness and Sobriety"

We will discuss the "modest apparel" in detail later, but surely the indication is that a retiring modesty of face is appropriate for a Christian woman. She should not be bold or loud-spoken or silly.

Doubtless this would imply that a Christian woman ought to dress conservatively. Certainly she ought to dress like a Christian.

A woman fashion editor in a national magazine wrote the other day that the miniskirt certainly would not be proper for church services. But the good Christian woman is "in church" all the time, in the sense she is always before the Lord. And all that she does—whether she eats or drinks or whatsoever she does—she should do to the glory of God. And if a woman ought to be modest in church, she ought to be modest and conservative all the time.

Evidently a Christian woman ought to be able to blush. It would not even be a sin for a woman to be retiring and a little timid before the public. She should be loving, outgoing, and earnestly helpful, but since she is not to claim leadership over men, her dress and her attitude and her speech ought to be typical of her heart attitude, that meekness and godliness which is her real adornment.

3. Oh, the Christian Woman Should Be Adorned "With Good Works"

What a wonderful record we have in the New Testament of good women and their good works! There was the poor widow who gave two mites and thus pleased Jesus so much! There was Mary of Bethany who came to anoint Jesus with the precious ointment when He was at the house of Simon the leper in Bethany. How pleased Jesus was with her love and her humble and yet rich gift! Jesus declared that it should be told wherever the Gospel would be preached and so He had it put in the Bible.

And there were those women who came with Jesus from Galilee and ministered to Him of their substance (Matt. 27:55, 56). Was it one of those good women who made that seamless robe of Jesus, so beautifully picturing His unpassed and uncontrived righteousness? And Jesus was pleased when a poor, sinful woman came to weep over His feet and kiss His feet and wipe them with the hair of her head!

In Romans 16 Paul wrote, "I commend unto you Phebe our sister, which is a servant of the church which is at Cenchrea" (vs. 1). Oh, you must help her, Paul thought, "for she hath been a succourer of many, and of myself also." And go through that chapter and find how many women Paul greeted. Priscilla; and "Mary who bestowed much labour on us." And he sent greetings to "Tryphena and Tryphosa" (were they twins?) and Julia and the sister of Nereus and others.

There is a blessed place for good women in the work of God, but it is not a place of authority over men. But women were in that pre-pentecostal prayer meeting in Acts 1:14. Mary, the mother of Mark, was prominent in the New Testament church (Acts 12). Person to person, Christian women have the same blessed freedom in winning souls that men have.

Oh, but women in public would have that ornament of good works as well as the meek and quiet spirit.

III. THE BIBLE TEACHING ON JEWELRY AND COSMETICS AND WOMAN'S BEAUTY

Let me say again that I think God intended women to be beautiful and attractive. The varying attractive colors in women's hair and the eyes, usually colored to match, the texture of skin, the beauty of features and form, the grace of movement, indicate that God intended women to be beautiful. So we should not fall out with women who want to be attractive. And the Bible, we think, has a clear picture about that that can help us.

1. Jewelry Is Not Forbidden in the Bible

It is true that I Timothy 2:9, 10 has this instruction for women:

"In like manner also, that women adorn themselves in modest apparel, with shamefacedness and sobriety; not with broided hair, or gold, or pearls, or costly array; But (which becometh women professing godliness) with good works."

That passage does clearly say that a woman's real beauty is not to be considered in the beauty aids she uses outwardly. A woman's real adornment must be inside in her character and shown outwardly in her modest spirit and her Christian works.

Taken alone, that passage might indicate even that a

woman is not to wear jewelry and not to braid her hair, although the Scripture does not say so expressly. But the supporting and parallel Scripture in I Peter 3:3,4 makes this passage clearer, I think:

"Whose adorning let it not be that outward adorning of plaiting the hair, and of wearing of gold, or of putting on of apparel; But let it be the hidden man of the heart, in that which is not corruptible, even the ornament of a meek and quiet spirit, which is in the sight of God of great price."

Note carefully here that a woman's adorning is not "that outward adorning of plaiting the hair, and of wearing of gold, or of *putting on of apparel."* Now, if plaiting the hair is forbidden here, and if wearing of gold is forbidden here, then the putting on of clothes is forbidden, too! We know that that is not true. No, it is not wrong to wear clothes, and it is not wrong to plait the hair and wear gold. Only these are not the things that make a woman beautiful, and so they do not count as beauty aids compared with "the hidden man of the heart, in that which is not corruptible, even the ornament of a meek and quiet spirit." Thus, plaiting the hair and wearing of jewelry is not forbidden, although that is not a woman's real adornment.

Jewels are mentioned often in the Bible, and they are never forbidden.

When a servant of Abraham went to get a bride for Isaac and when God had answered his prayer and led him to Rebekah, then this servant of Abraham "took a golden earring of half a shekel weight, and two bracelets for her hands of ten shekels weight of gold" (Gen. 24:22). And again after the family has consented and Rebekah is to go to be the bride of Isaac, we read, "And the servant brought forth jewels of silver, and jewels of gold, and raiment, and gave them to Rebekah: he gave also to her brother and to her mother precious things" (Gen. 24:53).

About those good Christians who speak oft to one another of the Lord, the Lord says, "And they shall be mine, saith the Lord of hosts, in that day when I make up my jewels; and I will spare them, as a man spareth his own son that serveth him" (Mal. 3:17). The saints of God are His jewels!

That thought must have been akin to the thought that God had when He had the breastplate made for the high priest with twelve precious stones and the names of the tribes of Israel engraved on those stones (Exod. 28:15-29).

The good works of a Christian at the judgment seat of Christ are likened to "gold, silver, precious stones" (I Cor. 3:11). And Heaven itself has streets of gold and gates of pearl and the foundation stones are great precious stones! So gold and silver and precious stones and jewels do not have a bad connotation in the Word of God. And the woman in the parable of Jesus, who had ten pieces of silver and lost one of those which she wore, probably as jewelry on her forehead or as a necklace, was wise to prize it.

And there is nothing in the Bible against cosmetics. Sweet incense was burned in the Temple of God and God loved the smell of it when it represented the praise and prayers of His people. When Mary of Bethany anointed Jesus with that oil of spikenard very precious, the odor of it filled the house as the sweet perfume was poured out on the Saviour and He was pleased (John 12:3).

It was a custom of Bible times to wash the guest's feet and provide oil for anointing his head, and when Simon the Pharisee neglected these gracious courtesies, Jesus rebuked him in Luke 7:41-50. And Proverbs tells us of "the ointment of his right hand, which bewrayeth itself" (Prov.

27:16). So men in Bible times wore perfume or ointment, as well as did the women, and it was not rebuked.

So we would have to say that the Bible does not forbid cosmetics, perfume, face lotions, and such like.

Within certain modest limits, then, cosmetics and jewelry are not necessarily wrong.

2. But As Beauty Aids, Surely Hair Styling and Jewelry Are Minimized and Played Down. They Are Not the Real Adornment a Woman Needs

Thus, to be overly adorned or too obviously keeping up with the extremes of styles would indicate that the Christian woman thinks more of the worldly standard of beauty than God's standard, and that would be wrong.

Sometimes the pastor's wife, appearing often in public and trying to be a real help to her husband's ministry, tries to be in the height of fashion, but such a woman, however good her motives, leaves an impression of worldliness with her hair piled extravagantly high, with her eyes shadowed blue or green, with her lipstick too violently red, or her dresses too tight or too short.

It is not worldly, we think, for a woman to be beautiful and to want to be beautiful: but it is worldly for her to have the same standards of beauty that the world has. A Christian ought to have a better standard than a worldly beauty parlor standard.

If the hairdo, the jewelry, the face coloring, or lipstick, or mascara are too prominent, they obscure that meek and quiet spirit which is the real adornment a woman ought to have. And perhaps more important, it leaves the impression on younger girls that the real beauty is that outward conformity to the world, and always to leave such an impression would be sinful and wrong.

I think for a Christian woman to be obviously dowdy or careless of her dress or her hair would be wrong and would dishonor the Lord. It is not wrong to have her purse, shoes or belt, perhaps, to match in color. It is not wrong that a dress should be well cut and well fitted. Then the dress will usually be more beautiful if it is not intentionally too tight, too short, or too extreme. If a woman's real beauty is to be her meek and quiet spirit, modest apparel and sobriety, then she should be conservative in her dress, not flamboyant, not shocking, not extravagant in cost.

Surely a Christian woman, even if she has plenty of money, would not want to put to shame other good Christian women who do not have money for expensive wigs, expensive jewels, expensive furs and dresses. And surely a good Christian does not want to tempt young girls to think that genuine beauty is outward and is made by beauty parlors and expensive stores. So "costly array" is not the adornment the Christian woman should seek.

IV. MODEST APPAREL—MINISKIRTS? SHORT SHORTS? SKIN-TIGHT STRETCH PANTS? HOT PANTS? BIKINI BATHING SUITS? TOPLESS GOWNS?

Never in America was the need so great for plain Bible teaching and preaching to grow a conscience on modesty in America. And particularly in women's garments. The miniskirts are higher than ever, sometimes showing ten or twelve inches of thigh. The short shorts and hot pants are common. The bikini bathing suits are scantier than bathing suits ever were before. Skin-tight stretch pants are very popular with women. Topless evening gowns are regularly in the news, worn by waitresses in nightclubs and restaurants, and worn in some weddings.

And there is no doubt that this immodesty in dress goes along with the great wave of lewdness and adultery. There are more divorces than ever. Authorities say half of all the brides eighteen and under are pregnant before they marry. Professors, some of them claiming to be Christians but actually are infidels and immoral, teach that sex intercourse outside of marriage may be just as holy and pure as in marriage. The movies frequently show scenes of stark nudity, and there are magazines which regularly picture flagrantly nude bodies of both men and women.

There is a constant increase in crimes of rape. Venereal disease is rampant again after being brought largely under control a few years ago. Women are not safe at night on streets in America and sometimes are not safe in the halls of the public schools or subway platforms. And no intelligent person can divorce in his mind the immodesty and lewdness in women's dress and the increased vulgarity and lewdness and immorality among the people.

There is no doubt that in the Scriptures heading this chapter, God connects a woman's modest dress with her obedience and subjection to her husband and to other men in authority. Wherever there is a breakdown of the authority of fathers over their children and of husbands over their wives, there is an increase in lewd and immodest dress. It is a part of a wave of lawlessness. When order and discipline and authority break down in the home, they break down in the church, then they break down in the school and in society. The wild immodesty in dress we often see around us is a part of a lawless, criminal age, rebelling against God, against the Ten Commandments, against marriage vows, against the moral standards held by decent people through the centuries and based upon the Bible.

1. A Modest Covering of the Body Is a Part of Decent Godly Character

We should remember that in the Garden of Eden when Adam sinned, he felt properly a need for covering of his body. There was no one to see his nakedness but his wife and God, but he felt that decency requires a covering for the body of a fallen race of people. And God endorsed that view and in pity for Adam and Eve, who had made themselves coverings of fig leaves, God killed innocent animals and made garments of skin for them.

We remember that after the flood Noah planted a vineyard and drank wine and was drunken in his tent. Many think that Noah was caught unawares, that before the flood grape juice had never fermented and he had never known drunkenness. At any rate, it is clear that with drunkenness comes the breakdown of those inbuilt instincts of decency and those inhibitions that protect character. So Noah was drunken and naked in his tent "and Ham, the father of Canaan, saw the nakedness of his father, and told his two brethren without. And Shem and Japheth took a garment, and laid it upon both their shoulders, and went backward, and covered the nakedness of their father; and their faces were backward, and they saw not their father's nakedness. And Noah awoke from his wine, and knew what his younger son had done unto him" (Gen. 9:22-24).

It was wrong for Ham to see his father unclothed, and brought a curse.

In Leviticus 18:7 is the command, "The nakedness of

thy father, or the nakedness of thy mother, shalt thou not uncover: she is thy mother; thou shalt not uncover her nakedness." So, incorporated into the Mosaic law was this moral principle already binding that God requires people to cover their bodies and to wear decent, modest clothes before others.

We remember that when the children of Israel had Aaron to make a golden calf that the people drank and rose up to play, and danced naked around that golden calf (Exod. 32:1-6 and 25). Nakedness goes with drunkenness and idolatry and is itself a sign of rebellion against God, the immodesty of one who does not confess his sinful need of divine mercy and covering for his sin.

That Gadarene demoniac who was possessed of a legion of devils "and ware no clothes, neither abode in any house, but in the tombs," when Jesus cast out the devils and healed him, was found sitting at the feet of Jesus, clothed, and in his right mind" (Luke 8:27, 35). Those who get right with God put on their clothes. Nakedness is itself a mark of rebellion, a lack of sensitiveness toward sin and native vulgarity and immodesty which comes from a rebellious generation.

2. Women Are Not to Pattern After Men in Their Clothing

In Deuteronomy 22:5 is this command, "The woman shall not wear that which pertaineth unto a man, neither shall a man put on a woman's garment: for all that do so are abomination unto the Lord thy God." And we remember that the sharp distinctions which God insists on between men and women and the appearance, is emphasized again in the New Testament in I Corinthians

11:1-16. The man should wear short hair with no veiling between him and Christ. The woman should wear long hair as a veiling, indicating her dependence on, and her submission to her father or husband:

"For the man is not of the woman; but the woman of the man. Neither was the man created for the woman; but the woman for the man."

So the woman is presumptuous who gets out of her place. She should not act like a man, she should not dress like a man. Pants for women came along with liquor for women and cigarettes for women and women's insistence on equal authority in the home with men.

Recently a woman wrote me that she worked on a farm, and in milking cows and gathering fruit and vegetables she felt that slacks were much more modest than dresses. But women never talked that way until it got to be the style, set by the ungodly world, for women to wear slacks. In my boyhood, women worked on farms much more than they do now, and in riding horses and in picking cotton, it was the regular thing for them to dress modestly, with full skirts that came below the knees, and under those skirts were black bloomers. They wore heavy cotton stockings and they were as warm in winter and as modestly covered always as if they wore slacks and they did not look as sexy, as, of course, they did not intend to do. Obviously the woman who wears tight trousers intends to call attention to her feminine form, and it is not quite honest, or at least it is certainly naive, to call that modesty.

Let us remember that in the Scriptures about a woman's adornment God has clearly in mind that a woman is to remember her submission to her husband and that she is to reserve the beauties and sex attractions of her body for her husband and that she should not uncover them to entice other men, nor offer to give what she has no right to give to others.

3. To Expose or Emphasize Parts of a Woman's Body for Sex Allurement Is Sinful, Wrong

It is true that God wants a woman to look like a woman, but He wants her to look like a modest woman. It is true that God wants a woman to be distinctly a woman, but she ought to appear plainly to be a woman who saves herself for one man. For him she saves her caresses, the enjoyment of her body, and heart surrender and devotion. One who is a wife ought to have the adornment of a wife. One who hopes someday to become a wife to a good man ought to have the adorning that fits that modest heart, loyal to the one man to whom God gives her and not traitorously squandering on others what should be the joy and comfort of her husband.

What is the purpose of the lewd pornographic magazines which picture nude women in alluring poses? Is it not deliberate catering to the natural passions of men? Is it not deliberately inciting desire? What is the purpose of those restaurants and nightclubs that put on waitresses with topless gowns? Is it not to attract the lewd who come to enjoy some sexual feeling along with the food and drink? Are not the movies, nearly always made by fallen, immoral men and women—are not these movies that show naked bodies intentionally catering to the profane and lustful crowds in order to get their money?

Then we must honestly suppose that women who expose their thighs, their breasts, their midriffs and outline their forms in skin-tight stretch pants, do it intentionally to attract the desiring gaze of men. So that kind of clothing could not be called "modest apparel"; neither is that kind of woman a modest woman in the Bible sense.

You women who are so obsessed in following the styles, and care more about dressing like the worldly crowd than you care about being modestly decent in the eyes of God, what a wicked idolatry is that!

Obviously the purpose of the miniskirt is to expose more of a woman's body. Then it is not modest. Above I said that in a national magazine a woman columnist, writing on miniskirts, said that, of course, they would not be suitable for church. Why not? If they were modest apparel to wear elsewhere, they would be modest in church. But there is a sense in which every good Christian woman is in the presence of the Lord all the time, and modesty is an element of character not put on and off with one's clothes.

Many high schools require that skirts cover a girl's knees. And they make the simple test—girls kneel down and if the skirt does not touch the floor over the knees it is not long enough.

At Bob Jones University, I understand that girls are required to wear skirts covering the knees. To appear once without that modest apparel means demerits, and the second time means more drastic penalty. And in that great center of culture where the fine arts and classics and good manners and good character are stressed more than in any other university in America, how charming and how happy and how clean and good do these young people appear! Yes and how attractive and stylish too! We think that Christian schools everywhere, and dads and mothers in the homes, ought to have at least as good a standard as that.

One will hear foolish excuses: it is not easy to buy longer dresses for tall girls. That is all very true, but if the style were for long dresses, then women wouldn't mind some inconvenience to have longer dresses! There are seamstresses who make dresses, or there are hems that can be let out, or a fringe or a band of cloth may be added. Where people want to do right, they will find ways to be decent and modest.

Sometimes it might be more convenient for people to drink instead of being total abstainers, but people still ought to do right. It would often be more convenient for a girl or boy to go along with the naked lewd necking crowd without making a protest or without being different, but people ought to do right whether it is convenient or not. Good women who really value their modesty and long to please Jesus Christ can find ways to dress in "modest apparel" as God commands.

So for the Christian woman, shorts and hot pants are out. The halter set, the bikini swim suits, do not fit the picture of a modest woman "with shamefacedness and sobriety" dressed in "modest apparel."

And even if skirts cover the knees, they still ought to be modest. Why need they be skin tight? And when a woman sits down, why should the skirt, no matter how she tugs at it, come above her knees? Why not wear a skirt full enough not to specially emphasize the hips and thighs, and full enough to cover the knees and thighs decently when one sits?

Strangely, this will be to some women a very serious thing. It is so hard to break from the leadership of ungodly and lewd people, their fashions and standards and opinions.

I do not think that a woman ought to be dowdy. If other good women wear skirts simply below the knees, why should a woman feel more virtuous if she wears skirts to the ankle? I do not think that one necessarily needs to appear queer. Neither does one necessarily need to make himself or herself conspicuous. One does not need to be a Pharisee to be a good Christian.

But modesty in heart and loyal subjection to husband or father and to Christ and His commands will surely help a Christian woman to dress in modest apparel and thus have the Christian influence that she ought to have.

6/ *Start a Family Altar Today*

Set a Time Daily When the Whole Family Gathers and Reads Together at Least a Chapter of the Bible, Has a Circle of Prayer, Learns a Verse or Two

Stop Raising Hippies! Help Save America! You Can Guarantee All Your Children Will Be Godly, Christian Citizens Serving Christ

"And these words, which I command thee this day, shall be in thine heart: And thou shalt teach them diligently unto thy children, and shalt talk of them when thou sittest in thine house, and when thou walkest by the way, and when thou liest down, and when thou risest up. And thou shalt bind them for a sign upon thine hand, and they shall be as frontlets between thine eyes. And thou shalt write them upon the posts of thy house, and on thy gates."—Deut. 6:6-9.

By testing congregations all over America I have come to the conclusion that less than one out of ten fundamental Christian families regularly have a time of daily Bible reading and prayer together. And surprisingly, probably not more than one out of three or four fundamental Bible-believing preachers has such a daily family altar of Bible reading and prayer. That is so shocking that we feel we should urge pastors everywhere to help us, and we should set out to get 10,000 more families having a daily time of such devotions together.

How explicit, how positive, is the scriptural command above about having in the heart the Word of God and teaching it diligently to the children; when sitting, walking, lying down, rising up, carrying Scriptures on the body, writing them on the posts of the house and on the gates!

In the preceding chapter Moses had just recounted again the Ten Commandments which were first given in Exodus, chapter 20. At Mount Sinai the people had said to Moses:

"Go thou near, and hear all that the Lord our God shall say: and speak thou unto us all that the Lord our God shall speak unto thee; and we will hear it, and do it. And the Lord heard the voice of your words, when ye spake unto me; and the Lord said unto me, I have heard the voice of the words of this people, which they have spoken unto thee: they have well said all that they have spoken. O that there were such an heart in them, that they would fear me, and keep all my commandments always, that it might be well with them, and with their children for ever!"—Deut. 5:27-29.

Here is a promise that God made again and again to Israel, if they would have a heart to fear Him and keep all His commandments, "that it might be well with them, and with their children for ever."

That promise is as pertinent to us as to Israel. For in Galatians 3:9 Paul is inspired to say, "So, then they which be of faith are blessed with faithful Abraham," and verse

29 says it even stronger, "And if ye be Christ's, then are ye Abraham's seed, and heirs according to the promise."

First Corinthians 10:11 tells us about the things that happened to Israel: "Now all these things happened unto them for ensamples: and they are written for our admonition, upon whom the ends of the world are come." It is true that the Old Testament contained not only the moral law but the ceremonial law (the Jewish Sabbath in this case), and the ceremonial laws are fulfilled and are not required of us. But God's eternal principle is the same. Those who teach diligently His precious Word have a right to these promises. It is a way to guarantee that you have godly children, good citizens. The way to a real Christian home must include, as a major factor, teaching diligently the Word of God to the children and enforcing its commands.

What a shame that all over America we find hippies, rebels, school drop-outs, dopeheads, and youngsters from nominal Christian homes. We find sex immorality, the draft card burners, defilers of the flag, enemies of the police and of the government, hating their fathers and mothers from the same kind of homes. You who do not have a family altar and the definite impact of the Bible on your home life, are raising these hippies, which means the destruction of America, unless the trend is reversed. Oh, ten thousand Christian homes reading the Bible, loving it, being taught it diligently, memorizing much of it, with godly discipline, would mean that Christian families in America would be rearing presidents, senators, governors, university presidents and professors and preachers of great churches. If America is to be saved it must be by Christian homes where God can mold the lives of the people through the Word of God and Christian discipline and teaching.

I. THE BIBLE IN THE HOME THE ONLY HOPE OF OUR CIVILIZATION

Christian morality comes only from the historic Christian faith, the old-time religion. It comes from knowing and loving the Word of God.

More than a century ago religious convictions and influence had so declined in England that the country seemed about to follow the convulsions of the French Revolution. The Gospel was rarely preached in the state churches—the Anglican church. The clergy themselves were usually Deists, unconverted, unbelievers in the historic Christian faith and given to gambling and drunkenness and bribery. The government was corrupt on nearly all levels. Laborers were exploited. Little children were sometimes compelled to work twelve hours a day in the mines and elsewhere. Prisons were disgraceful. There were almost no hospitals, no homes for orphans and very little public education. Unrest and wickedness seethed everywhere.

And then John Wesley and his helpers were used of God to bring about a great revival. He preached to thousands in the fields. He was stoned, slandered, abused, shut out of the churches, yet thousands were saved, and a conscience of England revived. Those influenced by the Wesleyan revival helped lead in abolishing slavery and making decent laws in caring for the orphans and for the sick.

1. Why Democracy Fails When Christian Morality Fails

There can be no Bible morality without honest Bible preaching and teaching. The principle of democracy is a greatly loved principle, but there is one fatal flaw in democratic majority rule. When the majority of people get corrupt, then they pass laws to get what they can get without principle.

There are more poor people than rich people, so they pass laws to take away the wealth from those who have earned it and give it to those who didn't earn it. When the majority goes wrong, then there are more people who drink liquor than those who do not, so they abolish prohibition laws. Then when the majority is corrupt, and they repeal the laws against pornographic literature, divorce is made easy, and the majority begins to press for the right to murder unborn babies (abortion). When the majority is corrupt, then they vote that everybody must have free medicare, free social security, minimum wage, full pay for a four-day week, etc.

When people are corrupt, then instead of seeking to get their just dues, the labor unions seek to get all the money they can, for less work all the time. When people do not have holy convictions about morality, then they continually vote to spend more money, get the government further in debt, owing millions that can never be paid.

So, as in Greece and Rome and France and many other countries, a democracy without the morality of the Christian religion becomes corrupt, lawlessness becomes rampant, people's lives and property are not safe, and eventually some dictator comes along who promises the people security and law enforcement and he gives it, though he takes away their liberties.

2. Delighting in the Scriptures, the Key to Prosperity

Loving and obeying the Scriptures while avoiding evil

men is the secret of perfect success for the individual, as we learn in Psalm 1:1-3:

"Blessed is the man that walketh not in the counsel of the ungodly, nor standeth in the way of sinners, nor sitteth in the seat of the scornful. But his delight is in the law of the Lord; and in his law doth he meditate day and night. And he shall be like a tree planted by the rivers of water, that bringeth forth his fruit in his season; his leaf also shall not wither; and whatsoever he doeth shall prosper."

What a wonderful promise! Prosperity in everything one lays his hand to, if he avoids evil company and meditates day and night in the Word of God!

The same precious truth was given Joshua:

"There shall not any man be able to stand before thee all the days of thy life: as I was with Moses, so I will be with thee: I will not fail thee, nor forsake thee. Be strong and of a good courage: for unto this people shalt thou divide for an inheritance the land, which I sware unto their fathers to give them. Only be thou strong and very courageous, that thou mayest observe to do according to all the law, which Moses my servant commanded thee: turn not from it to the right hand or to the left, that thou mayest prosper whithersoever thou goest. This book of the law shall not depart out of thy mouth; but thou shalt meditate therein day and night, that thou mayest observe to do according to all that is written therein: for then thou shalt make thy way prosperous, and then thou shalt have good success."—Josh. 1:5-8.

But here in the Scriptures quoted in Deuteronomy we find that the same blessed promise holds good for nations and for peoples and families. The family that delights in the Word of God, loves it, teaches it to the children, meditates in it—that family will be prospered, the children will turn out to be moral, godly, good citizens, happy, successful Christians, the Scripture says. The Bible is the only hope for our civilization.

3. The Home Is the Only Place Where the Bible Can Be Taught as It Ought to Be

It is true that the people who regularly attend churches that have godly, well-taught, Spirit-filled preachers, learn a lot of Scripture from the preaching. But it is only fair to say that only a small proportion of Christians attend churches where there is regular teaching of the Word of God from the pulpit. At most, it would be only a text or a short passage of Scripture before the sermon. Those who do not study the Bible for themselves but depend only upon the preaching they hear are always woefully ignorant of the Word of God.

Good, sound Sunday schools do teach some of the Word of God. Actually, Sunday school lessons do not give more than a relatively few selected Scriptures for study in the year's time. Even in good fundamental churches where the teachers are well prepared, a thirty-minute Sunday school lesson once a week will never teach as much Bible as people need. The thirty minutes of Christian emphasis in Sunday school once a week cannot hold its own in influence against many hours of teaching in the public schools, plus all the influence of the TV, the cheap literature that is available everywhere, and the influence of evil companions.

No, the one place where the Bible can be fully taught daily and adequately is in the home.

Millions of people feel, as I do, that the Warren

Supreme Court, a left-wing court, in re-defining the laws of America, did great harm in limiting the matter of prayer and Bible reading in public schools. Separation of church and state, provided in our Constitution, did not mean that our founding fathers were against the Bible. They were simply against any state-controlled and compelled religion and insisted that there be chaplains to have prayer in Congress and in each branch of the armed services. Public officials are sworn in on the Bible, taking an oath before God. Our coins proclaim, "In God we trust." Both our national anthem, "Star Spangled Banner," and our national hymn, "America," call on the people to trust God to take care of America. It would be perfectly proper to have Bible reading and prayer voluntarily, without any denominational propaganda, in the public schools, according to our Constitution but not according to the Warren Court. I say, I think they were wrong.

However, the simple fact is that in most of America the churches could have released-time sessions for teaching the Word of God and they usually do not take advantage of the opportunity. And if the school had, let us say, fifteen minutes or thirty minutes a day for reading the Bible, there could not be detailed teaching on controversial points where there is great difference among Christians. Even if we had liberty, the Bible teaching in the school will not fill the need.

But what hypocrisy it is for Christian people to indignantly blame the action of the Supreme Court about no Bible reading and no prayer in the schools when they do not have it at home! There is no law to prevent you from praying with your children. There is no law to prevent you from reading the Bible in your home and teaching your children the Bible. And it is a poor kind of escapism to blame the courts for forbidding Bible teaching in the schools, when you do not sincerely care enough about it to have it in your own home.

The only place we can adequately teach our children the Bible, as it ought to be taught, is in the home. Let's have all the help we can from the Sunday school, the preaching, Daily Vacation Bible School, Child Evangelism and summer camps. It still remains that those who attend only these outside agencies will have only a smattering of Bible knowledge, and they will not have the wholehearted devotion to the Bible, when it is not valued at home and read and taught with holy zeal.

II. BUT IT IS THE COMMANDMENTS GOD EMPHASIZES HERE

Read again that passage in Deuteronomy 6:6-9. "These words, which I command thee this day" are those that should be in our hearts and those we should diligently teach our children. And the Scripture has just gone over the Ten Commandments and related commands. It is true that the principle of this Scripture applies to the whole Bible as we have it, not only to the part of the law that Israel then had. But here is a basic summary of all human duty as given in the Ten Commandments.

The first four commands, including the ceremonial command of the Sabbath which was applied to the Jews, refer to man's duty to God. We are not to make images, we are not to make idols, we are not to bow down to them or serve them, we are not to take God's name in vain. The last six commandments sum up our duty to all mankind. We are to honor fathers and mothers, we are not to murder, not to commit adultery, no to lie, not to steal, not to covet.

Rightly interpreted, as they were interpreted in the New Testament, they involve all morality and righteousness. Jesus summed them up as being some detailed expressions of the great commandment, that one should love God with all his heart, mind, soul and strength and love his neighbor as himself.

1. Then the First Basic Truths of the Bible Are for Morality and Righteousness

There is a good reason why God gave the law of the Old Testament before He gave the New Testament. Men are to know they are sinners before they feel the need for a Saviour. Though repentance and faith are the two faces of that heart decision that God requires to make one a child of God, repentance is always mentioned first when they are mentioned together. You face the matter of sin before you face the matter of forgiveness and salvation.

The home that establishes a family altar, then, must set out to stress the *commandments* of God, what a righteous and holy God requires.

2. That Means That in the Home, Parents Must Emphasize the "Thou Shalt Nots"

There is a foolish teaching abroad based on the Dewey philosophy of education, a philosophy of Satan, that you should never say "no" to a child, that you should never say "you must not." People foolishly say that if you didn't make it against the law to take dope, many young people wouldn't take it. They say that with a law against drinking liquor, more people would drink it. That simply is not so. It is true there is a tendency for rebellion against God and against the law and against right, against authority, inherent in the carnal human nature. Christian parents dare not cotton to that wicked nature. The Bible says, "Thou shalt not. . .," and the foolish education professors are not as wise as God. God said to Adam and Eve in the Garden of Eden, "Thou shalt not eat of the tree of the knowledge of good and evil." In the Ten Commandments God says, "Thou shalt not," about idolatry, about profanity, about murder and adultery and lying and stealing and covetousness and rebellion against authority in the home. The Bible philosophy must prevail in the home which has a family altar.

3. It Necessarily Follows That God's Authority in the Home Rests in the Parents and They Must Enforce His Rules

The command, "Thou shalt teach them diligently unto thy children," means that parents speak with certain authority. Pupils must respect teachers. Sons and daughters must respect fathers and mothers, and listen to them. Parental authority is involved in this family altar business.

Read again the commands about whipping children in Proverbs 13:24; Proverbs 19:18; Proverbs 20:30; Proverbs 22:15; Proverbs 23:13, 14; Proverbs 29:15, 17 and in Ephesians 6:4 where fathers are comnmanded to "bring them up in the nurture and admonition of the Lord." The word "nurture" in the original really means "discipline" or "enforced discipline." The Greek word used here is the one used for chastisement in several New Testament Scriptures. And in the same Mosaic law, Deuteronomy 21:18-21 provides that with a rebellious son who cannot be controlled the father and mother have a right to bring the matter to the elders of the city and demand that he be stoned to death.

Just as in Psalm 1:1-3 the blessings promised for those who meditate day and night in the Word of God are conditioned on their turning from evil companions, so here it is only fair to say that the blessings promised to those who teach their children the Bible are conditioned on the godly authority of the parents.

In this matter, of course, God intended the man, the husband or father, to be the ruler in the home. The wife is to be subject to her husband, as we learn in Genesis 3:16; Ephesians 5:22-24; I Peter 3:1, 2. Joshua, the head of the home, said, "As for me and my house, we will serve the Lord" (Josh. 24:15). God even provided that a man should teach his wife the Scriptures and answer her Bible questions. "Let your women keep silence in the churches: for it is not permitted unto them to speak; but they are commanded to be under obedience, as also saith the law. And if they will learn any thing, let them ask their husbands at home: for it is a shame for women to speak in the church" (I Cor. 14:34, 35).

There can be no godliness without authority. The authority of God, the authority of the Bible, the authority of parents, and the authority of government all stand or fall together.

III. "TEACH THEM DILIGENTLY"

So says the Word of God. These are strong words.

1. Give the Word of God Daily Priority in the Home

One who takes seriously the instruction in Deuteronomy

6:6-9 must be impressed that the Bible is not simply one item of many, is not a minor matter and not only a major one, but it is a controlling factor of the whole life of a home.

First of all, the Word of God, the commands of God, "shall be in thine heart." The commands of God should be memorized, not only in the mind but in the heart, the seat of affections. A devoted love of the Bible so that one memorizes much of it, is here commanded.

And then this Word of God shall be taught diligently to the children. Parents shall talk of the Scriptures "when thou sittest in thine house, and when thou walkest by the way, and when thou liest down, and when thou risest up." That means every problem that comes up in the home will be dealt with in the light of the Scriptures. That means even with the children that the commands, God's Word, the promises, the warnings must be applied day and night. And the Scriptures shall be bound on the parents' hands and as frontlets between the eyes. Even if that be a figure of speech, it means surely that parents shall keep visible somewhere a constant reminder of God's law and the commands of God. They shall be written upon the posts of the house and upon the gates.

Dr. G. Campbell Morgan tells us that when he married, he was very proud of his little home until his father came to see him. Proudly the young husband showed his father through the home, waiting for his comment. Did he like it?

The father simply said that one could not tell whether it was a home of a Christian or an infidel. Not a motto on the wall, not a Scripture verse, nothing clearly reminding one that this was a house of a man of God. Morgan saw the point and so placed mottoes and Scriptures on the wall of every room.

2. Christian Homes, Then, Should See That the Bible Is Read Not Only by Individual Members but Publicly as a Group to Learn, Memorize, to Comment

Then if we take to heart God's commands about the home, parents must supervise their children in memorizing portions of Scripture. Into the plastic minds and hearts of little children, parents must engrave, never to be forgotten, the Word of God. Children should learn, of course, the Ten Commandments, the Lord's Prayer, the Beatitudes; they should learn a collection of Scriptures on the plan of salvation, on the security of a believer, on prayer and its answers, on Christian love and fellowship, on praises to God, on dependence for daily needs and fellowship, on forgiveness and love and soul winning. Surely the family as a whole ought to memorize many whole chapters.

In our home all of us memorized Psalms 1, 8, 15, 19, 23, 24, 34, 37, 100, 121, 126, 127. We memorized Matthew 28, the resurrection story, and said it from memory every Easter Sunday morning at the breakfast table. We memorized Luke, chapter 2, the story of the birth of Jesus. We memorized John, chapters 1, 3, and 14; I Corinthians 13; Romans 8 and 12; Philippians 4. We memorized literally thousands of verses of Scripture.

That means that some of this work was done at the time of family devotions when we read the Bible, then it was followed up in individual devotions and study, and then when we came together either at the regular family devotions or casually at any time while we were together, we repeated for each other the Scriptures we had learned.

To teach the Scriptures "diligently" means to memorize, to drill, to enforce the Scriptures.

3. How Have a Family Altar?

Any serious effort to teach children the Bible and to be good Christians means a regular scheduled time, part of the family program every day.

What time is best? In our own home, Mrs. Rice and I found that the evening is not the best time. I was often engaged in preaching services. It was not convenient to keep little children awake late or to wake them up for devotions. Besides, it is far better to start the day with Scripture and prayer with the whole family.

We tried it before breakfast, but that interfered somewhat with the meal. Warm foods got cold, and the toast burned. We soon found that immediately after breakfast was for us the best time in the day. Everybody was required to be at breakfast. Everybody must take part in the Bible reading and prayer. As soon as they could manage to read haltingly, little children were allowed to read one verse when it came their turn.

The importance the Bible gives to teaching children the Word of God and His commands means that this time must be religiously kept, it must have an absolute priority over other more ordinary matters. When in our home one of our six girls sometimes said with dismay, "But Daddy we will be late for school!" I simply said that we had to have family devotions even if they were late for school, and warned that the next time they must get up in time. We had family devotions whether every girl had her hair combed, whether beds were made or lesson prepared.

Families simply will not keep up family devotions if other things are allowed to postpone it or if it is not made a part of the daily unvarying schedule. Character is not made up of holy vows and aspirations. It is made up of habits following those vows. One is not just a good Christian because he loves the Bible and intends to study it. One becomes a good Christian when the Bible becomes so much a part of his daily schedule that he feels he must not miss it and would be miserable if he did.

The Bible must have priority. Have family devotions even if you have company. Have family devotions on holidays, on Sundays. Have family devotions if some member is sick. Have family devotions if the alarm clock fails and you are running behind time. Only if the Bible is given a priority will it have the all-compelling effect of godliness and happiness in the home which God planned for it.

How should Bible reading be done? Sometimes the father reads the Bible aloud to others. That is good, but we think that not the best way. Young minds wander. A child might sit quietly but his thinking be miles away. So we found it best to read in succession around the table. We would read one chapter or if it were Psalms, perhaps two or more, each day. I would read the first two verses, then clockwise around the table every child would read two verses and back to me again; around and around until we finished the chapter. Thus everybody had to keep the place in mind to know when his turn came to read.

Occasionally Father or Mother should call attention to some verse that is especially good and suggest that a bracket be put about that verse, and memorize it and you should return to it the next day for review. Occasionally there ought to be brief discussion. "Grace, what do you think verse 13 means?" Or after the reading, "Elizabeth, what verse do you like best in this chapter?"

I suggest that the reading be in the King James Version of the Bible. So-called "modern language" versions are usually paraphrases and not very accurate and sometimes with liberal, inaccurate rendering. The King James Version is the Bible of the people. It has the most beautiful language. The idea that the language of the King James Version of the Bible is archaic, hard to understand, is rather silly. I taught Shakespeare to college freshmen and sophomores, and the language of Shakespeare is ten times more archaic and obsolete than is the King James Bible.

Enjoy the Bible. If Dad and Mother find it sweet and blessed and if the family regularly prays for God to be with them in their devotions, they will find it the happiest time of the day. Visitors who come to our home have again and again remarked years later that the happiest memory of their visit was the family devotions.

And then we would pray in a circle around the table. I would begin the prayer, then each one would follow in his own way, asking God for His blessing, asking help for the chores and duties of the day, asking for healing for someone who was sick, asking for help to win some particular soul, asking for help in the school work. Tiny children who cannot read the Bible can be taught a little memorized prayer so they can have part and soon they can pray from the heart.

And the family altar is a time also to praise good deeds, to rebuke quarrels, to settle problems. And besides, it means there is such close contact between parents and children that any time during the day (and sometimes during the night) a child will feel free to come to Dad or Mother for more prayer, or for help about a burden, or to confess a sin. There is no "generation gap" in the family where the authority of Father and Mother is clearly recognized and enforced, and where they have family devotions together.

How long will devotions take? Often not more than fifteen or twenty minutes; but what a precious time together!

In Jesus' Name, Start Today!

In every home where someone reads this, if you do not have a regular scheduled time of family devotions, Bible reading and prayer together, I beg you, begin today.

I suggest as follows:

1. That husband and wife talk it over and fully agree and select a time when the whole family can be together. Talk it over with the whole family. No child can veto it, but children might feel free to suggest any problem about the time. And then when it is settled, it is to become a settled matter, as unchanging as the law of the Medes and Persians! Everybody gets up in time or everybody leaves whatever other occupations in which they may be employed.

2. Start with reading one chapter. Perhaps you should start first to read through the book of Matthew. Read through the twenty-eight chapters on twenty-eight consecutive days. Or you may like to start in Genesis. Sometimes when one book is finished it may be well to skip to the Psalms or to another part of the New Testament for a refreshing change.

And then let us say frankly, the head of the family must simply stand up and require everybody to be present, everybody to take part. That kind of family devotions requires family authority in the home.

If you will set out to have family devotions regularly, I suggest that husband and wife decide and then as a committal fill out this form here and mail it to me. That will mean that you will feel you have committed yourself and that the matter is clear in your mind, and it will help me to know that you are setting out to have a really Christian home. I beg you to decide it and send me word today.

Dr. Curtis Hutson
THE SWORD OF THE LORD
P. O. Box 1099
Murfreesboro, Tennessee 37130

Dear Dr. Hutson:

Today we have decided to definitely now commit ourselves that we will undertake to have a daily time of family devotions, reading the Bible, at least a chapter each day with the whole family and with a circle of prayer.

Time preferred______________________________

Number of children in the family________________

With what book in the Bible are you beginning
the daily reading together? ________________

Signed: Husband____________________________

Wife____________________________

Address________________________________

____

7/ ABORTION
The Murder of the Helpless Unborn

It is the custom of Satan and of sinful men that as sin increases, so do advocates of sin. First, men guiltily break the laws of God, then they question if they are God's laws after all and if the Bible is really the Word of God.

First they reject Christ as Saviour and then, eventually, as they continue their sinful rejection, they say Christ is not really God anyway.

First they drink until enslaved by drink and then they tend to mock at teetotalers and "blue laws."

First they break God's righteous moral laws until sex is emphasized on every page, in every film, in nearly every advertisement; until half the girls marrying before twenty are already pregnant, and lewdness is common in the colleges and in general society: then "situation ethics" claims that free marital sex is good and moral if there is "love," and the old abominable adultery is now the "new morality."

So now a church can have dances for homosexuals, churches are open to rock 'n' roll hippie concerts, and university doctors are authorized to sell young women students "the pill."

For long centuries no decent person, and certainly no

respected Christian, advocated killing an unborn baby. Like all killing of people by individuals, it was murder. So said the laws of civilized nations. So said the Christian pulpit. So said the enlightened conscience of the world. But now—!

Now the godless hasten to make virtue of sin. Now that little one, a gift of God given to be loved and cherished, has none to defend it. An adulterous woman or girl is pregnant. Kill the baby! It will be good for the shameless woman's mental health! A lazy, luxury-loving, self-centered woman who never intended when she married to take on the God-given responsibilities of a home, becomes pregnant. What will she do? She hates the gift of God. She doesn't want to feed it, clothe it, rear it. Then go to a doctor, threaten suicide, and pay a good fee to kill the unwanted baby! The doctor needs the money, and greed stills his conscience.

Here is a hard-working man with a happy, big family. Sure, they can have only one car. Sure, they have to scrimp and save as did all of our fathers in those less luxurious but better times. But every child can go on and finish high school. Some of the girls perhaps earn money babysitting; some boys will carry paper routes. And any ambitious and gifted among them can work their way through college. But all the "planned parenthood" do-gooders, socialist left-wingers, the Mary Calderones, the socialists—all insist on teaching that woman that she should be sterilized; oh, it would be a crime to have another baby! How can she give it the luxuries that rich people give their children! And so people are taught that what God gives is abominable and the blessing is despised and virtue in America flees away.

Now when millions of women want to avoid the results of their continued adultery, or avoid the duties of normal wifehood and motherhood, we have a thousand "reasons" given for abortion, for the murder of the unborn innocent.

We will answer those excuses, God willing, a little later. Let us now consider: First, the plain Bible warnings and punishments for murder. Second, the fact that every child is a gift of God who ought to be received and loved and cared for. Third, the scriptural and legal fact is that the fetus, from conception, is a person, a living soul. Fourth, how foolish, unreasonable and insincere are the excuses of people for this sin.

I. REMEMBER GOD'S DEATH PENALTY FOR MURDER

1. Death Penalty for Murder Before the Mosaic Law

After the flood God blessed Noah and plainly said, "And surely your blood of your lives will I require; at the hand of every beast will I require it, and at the hand of man; at the hand of every man's brother will I require the life of man. Whoso sheddeth man's blood, by man shall his blood be shed: for in the image of God made he man" (Gen. 9:5,6).

Even before there were courts of law, even before there were kingdoms and organized nations, God had the rule, and it was to be enforced by kinsmen of the murdered, if need be, "Whoso sheddeth man's blood, by man shall his blood be shed."

The word "man" is used in the general sense for men, women, young people, children. In verse 5 it is, ". . .your blood of your lives." Isn't there life as soon as there is conception? Is not the unborn child alive even before there is any outward movement? Isn't there blood in the fetus? Does not abortion mean shedding of blood?

2. Death Penalty for Murder in the Mosaic Law Too

What God gave before the law, He incorporated into the Mosaic Law; so in Exodus 21:12 is the plain command, "He that smiteth a man, so that he die, shall be surely put to death."

In that same 21st chapter of Exodus, along with the passage commanding the death penalty for murder, verses 22 to 25 say:

"If men strive, and hurt a woman with child, so that her fruit depart from her, and yet no mischief follow: he shall be surely punished, according as the woman's husband will lay upon him; and he shall pay as the judges determine. And if any mischief follow, then thou shalt give life for life, Eye for eye, tooth for tooth, hand for hand, foot for foot, Burning for burning, wound for wound, stripe for stripe."

Scholars who wanted to prove that the unborn baby was not a person have used this Scripture to try to prove that injury to the prematurely born child was not punishable, but that evidently is not what the Scripture means. Verse 22 says, "If men strive, and hurt a woman with child, so that her fruit depart from her" (a premature birth or miscarriage) and yet no mischief follow:" that would mean, evidently, no mischief to the woman or to the child. Premature babies born after the seventh month often live. But it seems an honest interpretation of the verse would mean that ". . .if any mischief follow" (that is, to the mother or to the child) "then thou shalt give life for life." On this matter in the book, *Birth Control and the Christian,* Dr. John Warwick Montgomery of Trinity Seminary says:

Moreover, even on strictly exegetical grounds, Exod.

> 21:22-25 does not say what Dr. Waltke thinks it does. He follows the interpretation of David Mace over against virtually all serious exegetes, classical and modern, in claiming that the passage distinguishes between a pregnant mother (whose life has to be compensated for by another life if killed) and her fetus (unworthy of such compensation). But Keil and Delitzsch, after explaining that the passage demands *exactly* the same penalty for injuring the mother *or* the child ("but if injury occur [to the mother or the child], thou shalt give soul for soul, eye for eye, . . .wound for wound"), comment in a lengthy note. . . .

Note that "virtually all serious exegetes, classical and modern," including Keil and Delitzsch, explain "that the passage demands *exactly* the same penalty for injuring the mother *or* the child. . . ."

3. The Death Penalty for Murder Is Also Clearly Implied in the New Testament

Murder is mentioned often in the New Testament. In Luke 13:1-5 we read the teaching of Jesus on this subject:

"There were present at that season some that told him of the Galileans, whose blood Pilate had mingled with their sacrifices. And Jesus answering said unto them, Suppose ye that these Galileans were sinners above all the Galileans, because they suffered such things? I tell you, Nay: but, except ye repent, ye shall all likewise perish. Or those eighteen, upon whom the tower in Siloam fell, and slew them, think ye that they were sinners above all men that dwelt in Jerusalem? I tell you, Nay: but, except ye repent, ye shall all likewise perish."

Those Galileans, murderers, were put to death by

Pilate, and Jesus said that was the will of God. God Himself killed others by letting fall upon them the tower of Siloam and that was counted just.

We are told, "Whosoever hateth his brother is a murderer: and ye know that no murderer hath eternal life abiding in him" (I John 3:15). And in Revelation 21:8 and 22:15 we are told that murderers are kept outside the Heavenly Jerusalem. And in Romans 13:1-7 we are told that the ruler is the minister of God, that he bears not the sword in vain but he is a revenger to execute judgment on the sinner. That teaches that when a government executes a murderer, it acts as the agent of God.

4. Note That God Makes No Exception in Forbidding the Killing of the Innocent and His Punishment of That Sin

The Bible never excepts unborn children from the rule that killing the innocent is murder. The Bible makes no distinction between the old and the young in that matter. The Bible sets no time when the child becomes a person nor does it intimate that up until some certain time the killing of the innocent one is justified. Only in the case of Exodus 21:22-25 does the Bible specifically mention retaliation for the death or injury of the unborn child. But then there is no discussion about whether a child ten years old may be killed without sin or whether an older man of eighty may be put out of the way to relieve his family of a burden. There is no need for God to specify ages when He has made the general rule for all ages. If He makes no exceptions, we should make none.

5. God Has Put in the Conscience of Mankind Rebuke for Killing of the Unborn Child

In Romans 2:14-16 we learn that God Himself holds people accountable for their conscience:

"For when the Gentiles, which have not the law, do by nature the things contained in the law, these having not the law, are a law unto themselves: Which shew the work of the law written in their hearts, their conscience also bearing witness, and their thoughts the mean while accusing or else excusing one another;) In the day when God shall judge the secrets of men by Jesus Christ according to my gospel."

The conscience of the world on this matter of abortion is illustrated by the oath of Hippocrates. Hippocrates is called "the father of medicine" and for centuries doctors have taken his oath as a moral standard governing their work as physicians. Honest doctors take this oath. Many doctors have it framed on the wall of their offices. That oath says, "To none will I give a deadly drug, even if solicited, nor offer counsel to such an end, and no woman will I give a destructive suppository, but guiltless and hallowed will I keep my art." The very purpose in medicine is to save life not to destroy it. And in this matter the Hippocratic oath represents the conscience of mankind and decent people through the centuries whether they were heathen or Christian.

Throughout the world there is a conscience on this matter of killing the unborn. Of course men may sear their conscience; men may so fight God's speaking to them through their conscience that they sear their conscience, just as they fight God and still the warnings of the Holy

Spirit. But God does not impress the conscience of millions contrary to the teaching of the Bible. So we would judge that God's intended truth in the Bible and in the conscience of men to be alike. It is sinful murder to destroy the unborn fetus.

Dr. George W. Truett, famous preacher of Dallas, Texas, said:

> Take the story by George Eliot, where she tells of the fatal going astray of a young girl. Earth's saddest sight is that. Let angels veil their faces, and let crepe be put on the door of heaven, when a young girl thus falls into shame. George Eliot tells it in her own inimitable fashion, and then she describes the young girl putting to death the little child to which she had given birth, seeking thus to hide the shame and crime. She slew the little child out there in the hedge, and later she was apprehended and brought to justice and judgment, and kindly women got around the wretched and fallen girl, and sought to counsel and help her. She listened to them—listened as if in a trance—and when they would finish saying to her every kindly and helpful thing they could think to say, she would answer them with the wailing chant: "Yes, yes, I hear all that you say, but will I always hear the cry of the little child that I put to death in the hedge?" What is the great dramatist saying? She is saying that conscience lives, and that men must reckon with conscience.

Yes, and Eliot is saying and Truett is saying that this conscience is from God. The murder of the baby, the fruit of her adultery, was a sin. But she could never forget the cry of the baby.

Oh, yes, and women feel the same way when they help to put to death the unborn fetus.

In Jackson, Mississippi, in the midst of a blessed revival, a woman came to me, distraught. Why could she have no peace? She sang in the choir. She taught a Sunday school class. She tried to live for God. She had been converted, and yet one thing was always before her: Years before she had gotten a mercenary doctor to help her kill an unborn baby she didn't want. Fifteen or twenty years had not stilled the burning of her conscience. Wasn't that of God? Wasn't God telling her she was guilty of murder? She could be forgiven, and was, but conscience still burned about her sin.

The specialists tell of the trouble growing out of the liberalized abortion laws in London. Nurses were supposed to take the crushed and bloody mass of the infant, taken from the mother, and dispose of it. Or they were supposed to dispose of the wriggling, suffering little one moving for hours or kill it. And so nurses, troubled by conscience, were finding themselves unable to sleep if they continued that kind of work and were insisting on leaving their jobs. And I feel sure that any woman of moral and Christian standards, any woman who is open to the work of the Spirit of God, will find her conscience accusing her of murder if she takes part in stopping the little life that God intends to give as a blessing.

II. BABIES ARE A GIFT FROM GOD AND OUGHT TO BE SO RECEIVED

The Lord Jesus said that not a sparrow falls without your Father. He says, concerning His people, that the very hairs of your head are all numbered or counted. Jesus said that God noted and colored every beautiful wild flower. Well, surely, then, it is not hard to believe that no little child comes into being, no mortal soul is created, without the direct act of God.

1. That Is What the Scripture Plainly Says

Psalm 127:3-5 says, "Lo, children are an heritage of the Lord: and the fruit of the womb is his reward. As arrows are in the hand of a mighty man; so are children of the youth. Happy is the man that hath his quiver full of them. . . ."

Children are "an heritage of the Lord." God gives little children. Does not that mean that anyone who hates what God has given, who does not want to care for what God provides, is thus sinful?

I know that God has given the husband and wife a part in the matter of the creation of new life, but we must remember that there never could come into being a newly created immortal soul if God Himself did not give it.

2. How Often in the Bible We Are Taught That God Gave Children in Answer to Prayer!

We remember that Abraham and Sarah long wanted a child. And now when they were very old—Abraham nearing one hundred and Sarah ninety—we read, "And God said unto Abraham, As for Sarai thy wife, thou shalt not call her name Sarai, but Sarah shall her name be. And I will bless her, and give thee a son also of her: yea, I will bless her, and she shall be a mother of nations; kings of people shall be of her" (Gen. 17:15,16). Notice God said, "I will bless her, and give thee a son also of her." The child Isaac, in answer to long years of prayer, was given of God.

In Genesis 25:21 we find, "And Isaac intreated the Lord for his wife, because she was barren: and the Lord was intreated of him, and Rebekah his wife conceived." God gave the twins, Jacob and Esau. And when? When "the

Lord was intreated of him, and Rebekah his wife conceived." God gave the children at the time of conception.

Leah had children. Genesis 29:31 says, "And when the Lord saw that Leah was hated, he opened her womb." That is, He made her fertile and she conceived.

In Genesis 30:22 we read how Rachel, long barren, was given a child: "And God remembered Rachel, and God hearkened to her, and opened her womb. And she conceived, and bare a son." God "opened her womb." He gave the child at conception.

How wonderful it is to read in the first chapter of Samuel how Hannah pleaded with the Lord until God gave her the child Samuel. And in Luke, chapter 1, we read how, after long years, the Lord answered the prayer of Zacharias and Elisabeth and promised the birth of John the Baptist, and gave the child.

We read in Ruth 4:13, "So Boaz took Ruth, and she was his wife: and when he went in unto her, the Lord gave her conception, and she bare a son." The Lord gave conception as a result of the normal intercourse. The child was a gift of God, given at the time of conception, surely.

Children are the gift of God. That gift is given at conception. To destroy one of His love gifts surely is a sin.

And we have a right to believe that anybody who loves and trusts the Lord will find that God will provide for what He gives and make a way for happiness and success.

III. THE UNBORN CHILD, THE FETUS, IS A PERSON FROM CONCEPTION

Some people have very foolishly said that the fetus, that

is, the unborn child, up until perhaps the time of the sixth or seventh month when it might live if taken prematurely from the mother, is only a blob of flesh, perhaps no more than a tumor. But that is simply not true. The little baby is not a part of the woman's body. It is a separate life. All the child will ever become is already contained in the genes, in that little one, and put there in the union of the sperm cell and the female ova. It has already determined the sex of the child, the color of its eyes and hair, looks, special talents and gifts, etc. All that the child will ever have inherently of its own is there now. Both the mother and father have already given to the child every characteristic they can ever give, except those outward matters of discipline and training during the years of childhood.

I am saying that that little being is a separate life. It gets nourishment from the mother, first for a time from the lining of the uterus, then through the amniotic fluid and then through the placenta, but already within that little bit of flesh are all the nerves and blood vessels and organs and bones potentially it will ever have.

The truth is that even after a mother dies the baby could be taken by Caesarean section and might live, as has often happened.

1. The Bible Plainly Infers That the Fetus From Conception Is a Person, a Living Soul

In Psalm 51:5, David was inspired to say, "Behold, I was shapen in iniquity; and in sin did my mother conceive me." Now give attention for a moment to that tiny bit in the womb of David's mother. As it begins to take shape, David said, "*I* was shapen. . . ." It was David even then.

He said, ". . .in sin did my mother conceive *ME.*" When the conception took place, it was David who was conceived. The honest inference is that from the very time of conception it was the person who would later be known as David.

In Psalm 139 the Psalmist David was inspired to write again, "Thou hast covered me in my mother's womb. I will praise thee; for I am fearfully and wonderfully made. . . .My substance was not hid from thee, when I was made in secret, and curiously wrought in the lowest parts of the earth. Thine eyes did see my substance, yet being unperfect; and in thy book all my members were written, which in continuance were fashioned, when as yet there was none of them" (Ps. 139:13-16). Note carefully all the formation of the baby who became later David the psalmist, formed under the hand of God, but David said it was "*My* substance"; he said, "I was made in secret"; he said, "*my* substance, yet being unperfect"; he said, "all *my* members were written. . .when as yet there was none of them." It was David's body being formed, David himself thus curiously wrought in the womb of his mother. Any honest interpretation here must surely be that that tiny being being formed in the womb was David, David's substance, David's body. He was a person.

We find the same implication about Isaiah the prophet. In Isaiah 49:1, 2, 5 we read:

"Listen, O isles, unto me; and hearken, ye people, from far; The Lord hath called me from the womb; from the bowels of my mother hath he made mention of my name. And he hath made my mouth like a sharp sword; in the shadow of his hand hath he hid me, and made me a polished shaft; in his quiver hath he hid me. . . .And

now, saith the Lord that formed me from the womb to be his servant. . . ."

Note carefully that God called Isaiah from the womb and mentioned him by name. He was preparing him then to be a prophet. He says, "The Lord that formed me from the womb to be his servant. . . ." It was Isaiah, and God had even mentioned his name (vs. 1). The person was there from the beginning. He was potentially the great prophet. But God had all the plans made, and all the elements that would grow up in the body and mind of Isaiah were already there potentially from conception. If someone had caused an abortion and killed a little one, he would have been killing Isaiah, already called by that name by the Lord, already being fitted to be a prophet.

We have the same kind of teaching about Jeremiah, in Jeremiah 1:4,5: "Then the word of the Lord came unto me, saying, Before I formed thee in the belly I knew thee; and before thou camest forth out of the womb I sanctified thee, and I ordained thee a prophet unto the nations."

God knew the Prophet Jeremiah when he was in his mother's belly; God sanctified him and ordained him to be a prophet. If by an abortion the fetus should have been killed, it would have been Jeremiah who was killed. The mother would not have known his name but God had already named him. The mother would not know that he was potentially a mighty prophet of God, but God had so planned it.

I am saying that a fetus is a person, a living soul, from conception.

We are told that John the Baptist was "filled with the Holy Ghost, even from his mother's womb" (Luke 1:15). We are told that when Mary the mother of Jesus came to greet Elisabeth, "And it came to pass, that, when Elisabeth heard the salutation of Mary, the babe leaped in her womb; and Elisabeth was filled with the Holy Ghost" (Luke 1:41). Now, God had already planned all the details of the life of John the Baptist at the time he was conceived. The fetus of John the Baptist in the womb of his mother may not have understood clearly why he leaped at the sound of the voice of Mary, the mother-to-be of the Saviour, but God knew. Did not God count John a person, already named and already filled with the Holy Spirit, long before he was born? Then would you not call that fetus in the womb of Elisabeth a person, a living soul?

It is interesting to note here that when Jesus said in Luke 18:16, "Suffer little children to come unto me, and forbid them not: for of such is the kingdom of God," He was speaking in reference to "infants" brought to Him for blessing in verse 15. The term there for infants is the Greek *brephos* and Young's Analytical Concordance defines it as "a child born or unborn." Does that mean then that all the little ones who died before birth had an immortal soul and "of such is the kingdom of heaven," and they will meet us there? Surely that seems to be implied.

3. The Incarnation of the Lord Jesus Christ Proves the Fetus Is a Person, a Living Soul From the Conception

The Angel Gabriel announced to the Virgin Mary, "And, behold, thou shalt conceive in thy womb, and bring forth a son, and shalt call his name JESUS" (Luke 1:31). Note that the Lord Jesus Christ was a person, an eternal person, before His human body was conceived by the Holy

Ghost in the virgin womb of Mary. John 1:1 and 2 says, "In the beginning was the Word, and the Word was with God, and the Word was God. The same was in the beginning with God." So we cannot wait until that little fetus moves or is "quickened" or becomes completely ready for life outside the mother for it to become a person. What was conceived was the human body of the Son of God.

We are told about the Lord Jesus in Philippians 2:6-8:

"Who, being in the form of God, thought it not robbery to be equal with God: But made himself of no reputation, and took upon him the form of a servant, and was made in the likeness of men: And being found in fashion as a man, he humbled himself, and became obedient unto death, even the death of the cross."

When did Jesus take "upon him the form of a servant and was made in the likeness of men"? That began when the child was conceived, certainly. Do you think that Christ had not yet given Himself when that little body began to form?

Now remember, immediately after the announcement of the Angel Gabriel that she should bare "the Son of the Highest" Mary went to visit Elisabeth; and the infant John, six months along in the womb of his mother Elisabeth, leaped for joy at the presence of the Son of God! And Elisabeth called Mary "the mother of my Lord." The Son of God, just conceived, was then, personally in the womb of Mary. He was a person present in that forming body.

But if Jesus was thus taking on Himself humanity, He took it at conception. The fetus was a person, a living soul from the beginning.

4. The Husband and Wife at Conception of a Child Are Thus "Heirs Together of the Grace of Life"

In I Peter 3:7 is a strange and wonderful statement that the husband is to dwell with the wife according to knowledge, giving honor unto the wife as the weaker vessel "and as being heirs together of the grace of life."

Evidently, then, God means that He allows the husband and wife to be partners with Him in the creation of life. The child conceived and born is a living soul and not only the body but the life itself is created. The person himself living in the body is created.

But when is it that the husband and wife work together to bring into being this immortal soul and the body that goes with it? It is potentially at the time of intercourse and actually at the time of conception when the sperm and ovum unite and development of a living person begins. At that moment all the characteristics of the child are determined and all the characteristics that can eventually be in the body and personality of the child have already been created by the husband and wife at the time of conception. We understand, of course, that the child may be influenced and trained but the inherent characteristics are already there from the moment of conception. The "grace of LIFE," the Scripture says. Then *life* begins at conception of the child, for that is when the husband and wife combine in another living soul. That fetus is already a person, a living soul.

5. The Word "Soul" in the Bible Usually Means Person

Some people have an idea that after conception, perhaps

at the quickening or perhaps at birth, God gives an immortal soul to the little body. But they thus fail to see that in Bible terminology the word *soul* means *life*.

For example, in Genesis 46:15-27 we read words like these about Jacob, "All the souls of his sons and his daughters were thirty and three." That is, all the persons. About Zilpah and her sons we read,". . .and these she bare unto Jacob, even sixteen souls." And again, "All the souls that came with Jacob into Egypt, which came out of his loins, besides Jacob's sons' wives, all the souls were threescore and six." The word *soul* means person.

And so in the ceremonial law, when we are told that for certain sins a man's "soul shall be cut off," it simply meant his life should be cut off. So in Joshua 11:11, "And they smote all the souls that were therein. . . ." In Psalm 22:29, ". . .and none can keep alive his own soul," that is, his own person.

The same terminology is used in the New Testament also, in Acts 2:41, ". . .and the same day there were added unto them about three thousand souls." That is, about three thousand people were converted, joined the church, at Jerusalem.

In Acts 7:14, speaking of Jacob, Stephen says, ". . .and all his kindred, threescore and fifteen souls." First Corinthians 15:45 says, "The first man Adam was made a living soul." In I Peter 3:20 we read that at the flood "eight souls were saved by water." That is, eight persons were saved; their lives were saved.

So, when the little one becomes a life it is a soul, a person, in Bible terminology.

6. In the Laws of Most States the Fetus, or Child Unborn, Is to Be Treated as a Person

Thomas F. Lambert, Jr., A.B., B.C.L. (Oxon.) is the Editor-in-Chief of the American Trial Lawyers Association, was Trial Counsel in the Nuremberg trials, was professor of law in Boston University School of Law from 1946-1955. In the book, *Birth Control and the Christian,* he has a splendid chapter on "The Legal Rights of the Fetus." He tells us how, in 1884, a court in Massachusetts held that the fetus had no rights in law for damages. For a time other states followed that rule, but this eminent lawyer says that almost universal opinion of lawyers and the more recent decision of the court holds that the child is a person from conception.

On pages 378 and 379 he says:

> The fetus or child in the womb should be treated as a person *for purposes of tort law* whenever that is necessary to prevent injustice. In Thellusson *v.* Woodford, 4 Ves. Jr. 227,332,31 Eng. Rep. 117 (1798, 1799), answering a disdainful contention that a child *en ventre sa mere* was a nonentity, Justice Buller said, "Let us see what this nonentity can do. He may be vouched in a recovery, though it is for the purpose of making him answer over in value. He may be an executor. He may take under the Statute of Distributions. He may take by devise. He may be entitled under a charge for raising portions. He may have an injunction; and he may have a guardian." In appropriate cases, the criminal law protects the unborn child and regards it as a separate entity. See, *e.g.*, Clarke *v.* State, 117 Ala. 1, 23 So. 671 (1898) (child born alive died as result of criminal beating of mother; *held,* murder of child). The law of wills and property, as indicated above, considers the fetus in being for purposes which are for its benefit and where justice so requires. As Dean Prosser

> sums up in his discriminating discussion of the point, "All writers who have discussed the problem have joined in condemning the old rule, in maintaining that the unborn child in the path of the automobile is as much a person as the mother, and in urging that recovery should be allowed upon proper proof."

Mr. Lambert admits that in most legal systems, expediency and justice indicate that "legal personality may begin or be assigned at live birth," but he says, "It is emphasized that *for purposes of tort law* protection of the child *in utero* may well commence from the moment of conception." The child, as a legal personality, cannot go to law for himself until he is born, but *"for purposes of tort law* protection of the child *in utero* may well commence from the moment of conception." A child is a person from conception according to legal definition.

The Encyclopedia Britannica under the item abortion says, *"In all the countries of Europe the causing of abortion is now punishable with more or less lengthy terms of imprisonment. Indeed, tendency in continental Europe is to regard the abortion as a crime against the unborn child."* The fetus, the unborn child, is a person.

7. Laws Against Abortion Around the World Show That Legally, Killing a Fetus or Unborn Baby Is Destruction of a Person, Is Murder

Does someone say that the unborn baby, the fetus, is no more than a bit of the woman's body, no more than a tumor, or an organ? Then why is it that there is no law against removing a tumor, no law against removing tonsils, no law against a hysterectomy, which means removing the uterus and ovaries of a woman when necessary? Why is it there is no law against removing a diseased kidney, or a gangrenous leg?

You see, the universal sentiment as expressed in laws around the world is that the fetus is a person and not simply a bit of the mother's body. No sensible person believes that it is only that.

Even the more liberal abortion laws still concede that abortion must be limited, controlled, perhaps sanctioned by two or three physicians. It must not be allowed after the twenty-fourth week of pregnancy. Without saying so, all those who want to make abortion on demand legal thus admit that it would take a law to make abortion permissible. The killing of a fetus is not like the removal of any organ or part of the body. The fetus, the unborn child, whether it could survive outside the mother's body or not, is regarded as a person.

IV. CONSIDER THE EXCUSES, THE INSINCERE ARGUMENTS OF THOSE WHO ADVOCATE ABORTION

New York State recently passed very liberal abortion laws. When the pregnant woman and physician agree that abortion is desirable, it is done. In the first six months, under the new law in New York State, there were 66,000 cases of abortion registered and done legally. In the first year there were over 100,000 in New York State alone. More lives were destroyed in the state of New York alone, under legalized abortion, than all the American boys who have died in Vietnam in years of war! Now, does anybody really believe that all these people or even the majority of them had Christian and ethical and moral reasons for wanting to destroy the little life God had given?

Consider what they wanted. They wanted the little skull to be crushed, the little body dismembered and removed from the womb and then disposed of. Or they wanted to have the little one's life-supporting amniotic fluid drained out by a hypodermic syringe and then replaced with brine to pickle the little one and kill it so, after painful threshing about, the dead body would soon be ejected. Or, if removed by Caesarean operation, then they would want the little one strangled or drowned or left to thrash arms and legs, struggling for hours before dying, as they sometimes do, we are told. (We read of such an aborted baby in Los Angeles that lived eleven hours, and we were told that some indignant people picketed the hospital. And some nurses in London rebelled, heartsick, because they were expected to finish killing the abortive babies or to watch them die and then dispose of the bodies.)

Do you believe that the reasons given were moral, ethical, Christian reasons for wanting the death of the little one?

1. Many Advocate Abortion "to Save the Life or Health of the Mother"

Now, suppose we admit that in a very few rare cases, probably not more than one in hundreds of thousands, the doctor must choose between saving the life of the baby and saving the life of the mother. I have never known of such a case, but let us suppose that is sometimes true. That would be a choice someone would make, just as if a man in a canoe finds it overturned with himself, his wife and baby and he must choose whether he should rescue and take to shore the mother or the child. He might choose to save one but he would not set out to deliberately kill the other.

Does anybody think that by killing the unborn child the mother's life is saved? The simple truth is, as thousands of doctors have testified, normal childbirth is safer than an abortion after the first few weeks of pregnancy. It is true that with specially trained doctors and hospitals, special equipment and nursing care, ordinarily an abortion can be performed and the little one killed and removed without much danger to the mother. But it is also true that if the abortion is in unskilled hands, if there is not adequate care, there is great danger of infection and danger of making the woman sterile, unable to bear children, and danger to the woman's life itself.

An abortion, to be safe, ought to be in a good hospital, with a specially trained physician, and special care.

However, millions of good women have borne children safely in their homes with ordinary sanitary precautions. In many cases, the baby comes too quickly for the pregnant woman to get to the hospital and the husband or the ambulance attendant or a policeman delivers the child and no harm is done. In other words, normal childbirth is natural and is not ordinarily dangerous to the life of the mother. Abortion is not natural, is more dangerous, and it takes more safeguarding. It is foolish and it seems to me insincere for anybody to suppose that in ordinary circumstances abortion is done in order to save the mother's life. That simply is not true and any such claim is not honest or medically intelligent.

Dr. Roy S. Heffernan of Tufts University said to the Congress of The American College of Surgeons, "Anyone who performs a therapeutic abortion is either ignorant of modern methods of treating the complications of pregnancy or is unwilling to take the time to use them." According to Dr. Joseph P. Donnelly, former Medical Director of Margaret Hague Hospital, New Jersey, "Abortion is never necessary to save the life of the mother." There were 115,000 deliveries at this maternity hospital from 1947 to 1961, during which time no abortions were done. Those who advocate abortion to save the life of the mother are either ignorant or insincere.

2. Abortion Is Advocated "if Childbirth Would Endanger the Mother's Mental or Physical Health"

Note carefully that term "mental health." In other words, if the woman would be unhappy to have a child, then her "mental health" is affected. And so, ordinarily, when liberalized abortion laws are passed, they require that the attending physician should have the sanction of two other physicians, one of whom would be a psychiatrist!

If a woman simply does not want a child, does that mean that her health is endangered? If instead of the baby she wants to spend her time in social affairs or in political campaigning, or if she wants the income of a job and the pleasure of a second car, instead of the baby, does that mean that her "mental health" is endangered by the child? Does anybody suppose that the woman with only one or two children is mentally more healthy, is happier, is better balanced than the woman with five or six children? Does the woman who has her baby murdered really have better mental health than Susannah Wesley with nineteen children? Or my mother who had five?

Do you believe that those 66,000 women in New York State who helped kill their babies in the first six months of legalized abortion laws were really doing that to maintain their mental health?

It is true that when the baby is illegitimate, when a girl has gone into sin and will be shamed by bearing a child out of wedlock, there will be some mental suffering in the disgrace. It would be shocking and contrary to good morals if one were not ashamed of adultery and license. But will adding murder to adultery make the wayward girl or woman more happy? More than one woman has talked to me after having been a party to abortion of unwanted babies.

Women have come or have written to me in deep distress long years after their sin, wanting my counsel and prayers that they might have peace for their guilty consciences. Would one advise a life of crime to ease the guilty conscience of the first offender? Or would you advise adding this crime of murder of the innocent to adultery to ease the guilty mind of the fallen girl or the adulterous woman? It is not proved to be so.

Dr. Ben Sheppard of Miami, nationally known physician, attorney, Juvenile Court Judge, lecturer, writer, and Chairman of the National Council on Crime and Delinquency, says, "Young adolescents who have had abortions may verbalize relief to please adults, but this is never their internal feeling. Their psychic trauma and loss of personal morality will persist throughout life." And Dr. John L. Grady, the obstetrician, of Belle Glade, Florida, who has delivered thousands of babies, says: "There are many cases where the mother has spoken of abortion early in pregnancy and later on has confessed her gratitude to the physician for not having performed the abortion, and has expressed great happiness when she sees the fruit of her pregnancy. On the other hand, I have studied case histories of married women who have become troubled, consumed with guilt and developed significant psychiatric problems following, and because of, abortion. I believe it can be stated with certainty that abortion causes more deep-seated guilt, depression, and mental illness than it ever cures."

Dr. Forrest C. Stevenson, Certified Marriage Counselor, of Brighton, Michigan, says: "As a marriage counselor, I have too often shared with a couple in this sorrow. They love each other, but as they look at each other, I see the hurt in their eyes. I've heard the woman say, 'Seven years ago my husband said I could not have this baby. "I'm still in school, I'm going to get my education first." I did what he said and I had an abortion. I wonder what that baby would have been like. Would he have had curly hair like his daddy? Would he have been a happy baby? Would it have been a girl? Would it have been a boy? What could have happened?'

"Too many times I've heard a young man say, 'I demanded that my wife get an abortion, but I wish that she had not done what I said.' These people may love each other, but the hurt of a guilt that they share together has grown like a wall between them. It is so serious that they can hardly build an adequate life. Their marriage is a nightmare because of a shared guilt."

It is not good for anybody's mental health to murder anybody and the murder of the innocent unborn does not give peace of mind to a troubled woman.

Some have claimed that liberalized abortion would save many a troubled woman from suicide. The simple fact is that detailed investigation by physicians and others have shown that pregnant women are no more likely to commit suicide than are others and those with illegitimate pregnancies no more likely to commit suicide than are others.

The right answer to sin is repentance and trusting the Saviour for forgiveness and for rearranging the soiled life. To add sin to sin is not the way to peace nor "mental health."

3. Abortion Is Advocated When It Is Thought That the Child May Be Handicapped or Imperfect in Body or Mind

It is true that when a pregnant woman in a certain month of pregnancy has rubella (German measles), the unborn child may be affected. A beloved young girl I know was born deaf, we think, because her mother had German measles before the child was born. I have known of one other case where a child was born with only one foot, and I have known another case where the hands and arms were smaller than usual and imperfect, though useable. It is supposed that these deformities were caused by some injury to the mother during pregnancy and possibly by German measles. And certain kinds of tranquilizers have been known to retard the development of unborn children.

But it is said by some physicians that the likelihood of physical imperfection or deformity in a child, when the mother has German measles during certain months of pregnancy, is only one to five. Other authorities say probably only one in ten. Suppose you knew that in five cases where mothers had German measles during certain months of pregnancy, one of the five would be defective in hearing (the most probable defect) or have some other minor imperfection in the body. Would you say that we ought to murder all five of the babies just to make sure that one was not born deaf? In that case, wouldn't it be better to wait until they are born and one is proven to be deaf, then kill that one rather than murder all the other helpless ones? You are shocked at the thought of murdering one little deaf child, but why not be shocked at the thought of murdering all five in order to kill the deaf one?

But suppose it could be proved and that one knew ahead of time that a certain child would be deaf or born with one arm or even be mentally retarded? Does that little child have no rights because it is imperfect? And even the one who is mentally retarded, and can never be brilliant, perhaps never be quite normal—do you think it is right to kill such and deprive him or her of life? Did not God Himself give the person the soul? And if it is right to kill the fetus before it is born because it might be defective, wouldn't it be just as logical to kill those already born who are defective? Or a burden to society?

4. Abortion Advocates and Insists That the Fetus, at Least Before the Twenty-fourth Week, Could Not Survive Without the Sustenance and Protection It Gets From the Mother's Body, That It Thus Has No Personality of Its Own, No Contacts With Others Who Would Grieve at Its Loss

The simple truth is that a baby, after it is born, cannot live without care and sustenance from the outside, also. The baby is dependent on others just as truly as the unborn fetus is dependent upon its mother. And in any normal motherhood, with godly Christian women who have a Christian philosophy of life, the baby is loved from the time the mother knows she has conceived and she feels that the little one belongs to her and God is working some changes in her heart, during the months of gestation.

So the baby could not live by itself? Well, it is also true that some paralyzed people cannot live without a lung machine that constantly works mechanically to keep them breathing. Other people wear a little electric regulator whose impulse keeps the heart beating regularly. Would it be proper then to kill them because they cannot live without help?

A quadruple amputee comes back from the war—no arms, no legs. Unless someone feeds him, he cannot live. Is he then not a person? Does one think it would not be murder to kill him since he is dependent on others?

A person injured in an accident lies in a coma. He cannot live without the glucose which is steadily fed into his veins. He is as dependent on others as is the unborn child. Do you say he has no rights of his own?

You see, the truth is that those who now advocate the murder of any unwanted baby will later be advocating, as did Hitler, the murder of others who are "unfit," or "retarded," or those who are an extra burden to society.

5. Some Advocate Abortion to Prevent Large Families Where, They Say, Another Child Would Add to the Financial Burden and the Cares of the Home

It is true that a large family eats more food than does a small family, that eight children need more clothes than do four children. But it is also true that there are other greater blessings that go with larger families. Any well-reared child, given by God and received as a blessing from God and reared for God, is a continual blessing to father and mother and others.

And it is also true that when God has given a child, honest, good people who do right can have God's help in taking care of the little ones. How long in all the world that has been proved true!

It is true that with drunkenness or extravagance, people are not always able to take care of the children adequately. It is true that the family with many children may not be able to have two or three cars, they may not be able to take a winter vacation to Florida, or a vacation to the ski country, or a trip to Europe. It may well be that the children cannot go to college with all expenses paid and without skimping and working and planning and scheming to get through. But it is also true that happy families do not necessarily need a winter vacation in Florida nor a summer to travel abroad. It is true that not all children ought to go to college, and those who want to badly enough can go, no matter whether the family has money or not. So I went to college and so have literally thousands of others. The truth is that people who want luxury and do not want the cares of a family thus make a false excuse.

IV. ABORTION IS A SIN

The killing of the unborn baby is a sin. This is a moral question. It is on the same basis as the murder of the incompetent, the retarded, the handicapped, the senile aged. It is probable that ninety per cent of the children born were not wanted at first, but they usually win their way into the hearts of parents. Is it right to kill the unwanted?

To despise and refuse the gift of God is a sin. To slay the

innocent because he cannot protest nor swear out a warrant is a sin. And the Scripture says, ". . .be sure your sin will find you out" (Num. 32:23). There is a God who cares for the weak, the unloved, the unprotected. He will bring judgment.

If some Christian has been guilty of this sin at the judgment seat of Christ when one must "receive the things done in his body, according to that he hath done, whether it be good or bad" (II Cor. 5:10), there will surely be an accounting for this sin. One does not sow without reaping. One does not mock God or injure His little unloved ones and get by.

At the great white throne judgment when the unsaved are gathered, souls out of Hell and bodies out of the graves and the sea, there will be many who will come to witness against the lost along with the men of Nineveh as Jesus promised. And then the souls of these little innocent ones, betrayed and murdered when they were intended to be a cherished blessing, will appear to accuse their murderers.

This question cannot be settled aright except as a question of right and wrong.

Dr. Forrest C. Stevenson, Certified Marriage Counselor from Brighton, Michigan, says:

WHERE DO WE GO FROM HERE?

If the abortionists win their cause in America, where do we go from here? Nazi Germany enacted a law permitting the elimination of "useless" members of society, people who were seen to be of no value to society. Of course it was aimed at the Jews and other non-Aryans. In the ensuing years over eighteen million people were slaughtered because they represented a category of human beings who were "useless."

Now we have the same pattern coming in America in which

a whole category of humans, unborn babies who cannot yet speak for themselves, are to be slaughtered at the whim of a mother and a doctor who signs that the mother is somehow unable or unwilling to have a baby.

Where do we go from here? What is the next class of humanity to be destroyed? Is it going to be the aged? This would certainly solve the problem of providing housing for the aged.

Is it going to be the incurably ill? Somewhere, someone has an uncle dying of cancer and he'd just love to get that uncle out of the way so he can take over the estate.

Is it going to be the mentally ill? the mentally retarded? Is it the racial minority?

Where do we go from here? It is going to be Christians? Now I don't have to be very paranoid to face what history has shown in the past and what is proposed by the abortionists, and say **this is an abomination.** It is an abomination.

Listen to me, Doctor: the Bible says, "Cursed be he that taketh reward to slay the innocent person." Cursed be he. Listen, "Who so sheddeth man's blood, by man shall his blood be shed, for in the image of God made he man." I speak for the innocent, for the unborn, for the one who cannot speak for himself. This one who is going to be an individual never duplicated again in all of human history. I speak for that unborn today. Tomorrow it may be any other "useless" category of human beings.

Dr. Stevenson also says:

I discussed this recently on a radio program, and had a phone call from a doctor who wanted to talk to me. That night we talked for a long time. I can share just a few things. He told me of his first abortion when he was a third-year medical student. I'm not going to go into the details of why: his financial hardship and other problems that brought him to do this thing.

After he performed this abortion, he told how he became so

> violently ill that he thought he would die. He went through weeks of depression when he thought of suicide. He said, "The first time I felt like a murderer, but I did it again and again and again, and now twenty years later—for the first time in all these years—I am again facing what happened to me as a doctor and a human being. Sure, I got hard. Sure, the money was important, and oh, it was an easy thing, once I had taken this step, to see these women as animals and these babies as just tissue."

All over America have gone out form letters announcing that certain persons will arrange for abortions, including the doctors in hospitals, etc., in New York State. One woman, walking about in an airport with a loose-fitting coat so that she might be thought pregnant, was approached by four different people offering to lead her to a doctor who would be glad to perform an abortion. Doctors are human beings, and one doctor plainly says, "It is dead babies for dollars; that is the name of the game."

There ought to be all over America a mounting indignation against those who murder the unborn, against the doctors, who for money, thus violate the Hippocratic oath, and set out to take life instead of preserving it. Open protests in the newspapers, socially shaming the guilty, preachers making an issue in the pulpit, editors everywhere protesting ought to help rebuild the conscience of America.

It is not surprising that the people who are eager to legalize abortion and murder more unborn babies, are the same crowd that do not want the death penalty for murder in other criminal cases. They are usually the same crowd, the left-wing, the demonstrators, the socialists, the civil rights lawbreakers. They are against censorship of pornographic literature and filthy movies. They are for the "new morality" and license. The people who are strongest for abortion are not good people and they are not good citizens of America.

8/ Don't Let Satan Get Your Children

Bible Example Shows the Tragedy of Godly Parents Having Wicked, Godless Children. But God Has a Guaranteed Way of Success in Rearing Children

"Train up a child in the way he should go: and when he is old, he will not depart from it."—Prov. 22:6.

It is a shocking thing that Christian parents often utterly fail in rearing godly children.

Whence come all the "new generation," the "revolutionaries," the demonstrators, the draft-card burners, the drug "honkies," the rock-'n'-roll generation, the school dropouts and rebels? Whence come the girls pregnant before marriage, the young people in premarital sex in college dormitories and parked cars, at the seaside or in apartments? Shockingly, they come, many of them, not only from respectable, moral homes, middle class and even luxurious homes, but often from homes of Christian parents. Why?

A man forty years old was converted in the rescue mission in Evansville, Indiana. He told me he was the son of a godly Methodist preacher. A famous missionary wept in the presence of my brother about his unsaved, unbelieving, skeptical son and daughter. One of the greatest fundamental leaders in America wept as he heard me preach on Lot and *The Ruin of a Christian,* and he told me later, "If my home had been what it ought to be, surely my children would be serving the Lord. They are not."

The arrest of Billy Sunday's sons for drunkenness was a recurring scandal. The gifted son of a great Southern Christian leader showed much promise, with a sweet singing voice and earnest preaching. But in a seminary he came to not believe the Bible, he began smoking, he attended the movies, and then eventually he gave up all plans to preach the Gospel and serve God.

A famous Bible teacher, with seven or eight children, was brokenhearted that only one of them nominally served the Lord.

Karl Marx, of a Jewish family, was baptized as a Protestant. Joseph Stalin was educated in a religious seminary and was intended for the priesthood.

When I have preached in jails all over America, I have found men who insisted their parents were devout Baptists or Methodists or Presbyterians or Pentecostal people or Catholics. To a shocking degree, the rebels, the immoral, even the criminals, come from homes of Christian parents. That is shameful but true.

Is the so-called "generation gap" inevitable? Must parents lose communication and control over their children? No, they need not! The plain promise of God's Word in Proverbs 22:6 is, "Train up a child in the way he should go: and when he is old, he will not depart from it."

Sometimes people have foolishly said, "No Christian can ever tell how children will turn out." Yes, one can tell if a godly father and mother set out to turn the children out on the Bible plan.

There is an old folk saying, "When the children are little, they tromp on your toes, and when they are older, they tromp on your heart." But my children never did tromp on my toes when they were little, and they do not tromp on my heart now that they are older.

Oh, I beg you Christian people, do not lose your children! You need not!

I. TRAGIC EXAMPLES OF BIBLE CHRISTIANS WHO LOST THEIR CHILDREN TO SIN

We are not surprised to find in the Bible, as in life about us, the children of wicked, godless parents often followed in the sins and in the punishment that always falls on the unrighteous. But it is a sad truth that often godly parents in the Bible did not so rule and train their children, did not bring them up in the way they should go, and so their children did not serve God. Often sin, disgrace, heartbreak and punishment came on the rebellious and wicked children of righteous people in the Bible.

1. Lot: His Home a Failure, His Religion Mocked, His Children Wicked

One of the saddest stories in the Bible is about Lot. It is the story of the ruin of a Christian. Oh, yes, Lot was a Christian man. In II Peter 2:6-9 Lot is called "just Lot," "that righteous man." He had a "righteous soul." He was "godly" and so delivered out of temptation.

Lot knew about God and came with Abraham when

God called him out of Ur of the Chaldees. He seemed to have lived with Abraham for a long time. No doubt he saw and perhaps took part in the sacrifices which Abraham offered. He knew about Abraham's contact with God. From the Scriptures we take it that he himself was trusting in God, was a godly, righteous man in his heart and wanted to do right.

There is reason to believe that Abraham did wrong in bringing Lot with him to the promised land, when God had commanded him, "Get thee out of thy country, and from thy kindred, and from thy father's house, unto a land that I will shew thee" (Gen. 12:1). His nephew Lot was "kindred," but Abraham did not leave him behind. No doubt God knew that Lot was not spiritually minded, would not be a help to Abraham but a hindrance.

We can see from the Bible accounts some of the failures of Lot that meant the ruin of his family.

First, he made an idol of his business, his flocks, his herds, prosperity. When his servants and the servants of Abraham strove over the limited grassland around their joint camp, then when Abraham offered him the first choice of the land, Lot selfishly chose the finer grassland, leaving his uncle in the more barren hills. Gratitude for Abraham's long supervision and care did not move Lot to be generous. The wickedness of the people among whom he moved did not deter him. Flocks and herds, money, prosperity, business were put first, and that was wrong, as it is wrong for anybody else.

"Lot dwelled in the cities of the plain, and pitched his tent toward Sodom. But the men of Sodom were wicked and sinners before the Lord exceedingly."—Gen. 13:12, 13.

The awful sex perversion, which is called today Sodomy, taken from the name of Sodom, did not keep him from joining in with these wicked men. When they would have raped the angels of God, Lot protested weakly but called them "brethren" (Gen. 19:7). Lest he should displease them, he would have consented to offer his daughters to be ruined by their lust. No one can rear children in bad company, giving them honor, friendship, disregarding their vices, without bringing a curse on their children.

No doubt Lot took up the habits of Sodom. Even when he fled from the city and lived in a cave, he had wine and he got drunk. The friendly contact with Sodom and the Sodomites left him with the mark of their worldliness, their loose morals, in his convictions.

The religious life of Lot is not discussed. Did he ever offer sacrifice? The Bible does not mention it. We suppose rarely, if ever, did he worship God, although he is called a righteous soul, called a godly man! His older daughters, we suppose, were not offended by the moral standards, the lewdness, idolatry, the wickedness of Sodom; so they married men of Sodom. The angels led the two unmarried daughters out of Sodom before it was destroyed, but they did not take the Sodom out of the girls, out of their conscience, their moral standards. Even Lot's wife was enamored of Sodom. She looked back longingly and was turned into a pillar of salt. When Lot went among the sons-in-law pleading with them to flee for their lives, they thought it was all a joke: "But he seemed as one that mocked unto his sons in law" (Gen. 19:14).

What a tragedy unspeakable in the home of a godly man! Wife turned into a pillar of salt, married children and grandchildren burned alive; the two single daughters, when all his property is gone and they live in a cave, get the old man drunk and commit incest with him and bear illegitimate children. O Christians, nobody has a right to let his family turn out that way.

2. Eli, the High Priest, Fathered Wicked Boys That Came to Awful Judgment

First Samuel, chapter 2, tells the story of Eli and his wicked sons. Eli was the high priest and was evidently a godly man. When Hannah prayed for a son, "Then Eli answered and said, Go in peace: and the God of Israel grant thee thy petition that thou hast asked of him" (I Sam. 1:17). One cannot argue that Eli was personally wicked or that he did not know the Lord.

But his grown, married sons despised the sacrifices and sent servants to demand what they would have of the sacrifices to eat; they would not obey the rules, would take by force what they wanted if it was not given to them. "Wherefore the sin of the young men was very great before the Lord: for men abhorred the offering of the Lord" (I Sam. 2:17). These wicked sons "lay with the women that assembled at the door of the tabernacle of the congregation" (vs. 22).

And the Lord quite clearly held Eli responsible for these wicked sons, saying to Eli, "Them that honour me I will honour, and they that despise me shall be lightly esteemed" (vs. 30). So a curse was pronounced on Eli's house forever; the two sons should die in one day and God said, "I will raise me up a faithful priest, that shall do according to that which is in mine heart and in my mind: and I will build him a sure house; and he shall walk before mine anointed for ever" (vs. 35).

Later, to the child Samuel the Lord said, "In that day I

will perform against Eli all things which I have spoken concerning his house: when I begin, I will also make an end. For I have told him that I will judge his house for ever for the iniquity which he knoweth; because his sons made themselves vile, and he restrained them not" (I Sam. 3:12, 13).

An attack came by the ancient enemy, the Philistines, and the elders of Israel took with them to the second battle the ark of God. But again the Philistines won and the ark of God was taken captive and the two sons of Eli, Hophni and Phinehas, were slain, as the Lord had prophesied. Eli fell, broke his neck and died at the news.

When the high priest of Israel, himself, lets his family go to ruin, that is a shocking warning to other Christian leaders.

3. King David Had One Son Who Was a Rapist, One Was a Murderer and Rebel, Another a Rebel. Why?

Among the noblest men in the Bible stands David. God called him "a man after my own heart." He was selected to be the ancestor of the kingly line of the Lord Jesus. To him were given, by divine inspiration, most of the Psalms. His devotion to the Lord, his following the leadership of the Holy Spirit in many matters, his answers to prayer, mark him as a man greatly blessed of God and greatly loved by the Lord.

Yet there is tragedy that stalks the house of David. One son, Amnon, raped his half sister Tamar (II Sam. 13:11-14). Tamar's brother, Absalom, hated Amnon and after two years he had the rapist murdered.

Then Absalom, disaffected, perhaps not quickly forgiven

by King David, became a conspirator, stole away the hearts of the people and then rebelled and set out to seize the kingdom and kill his father David!

After the rebellion by Absalom had been put down, David's kingdom restored to him, and David was an old and sickly man, we read:

> *"Then Adonijah the son of Haggith exalted himself, saying, I will be king: and he prepared him chariots and horsemen, and fifty men to run before him. And his father had not displeased him at any time in saying, Why hast thou done so? and he also was a very goodly man; and his mother bare him after Absalom."*—I Kings 1:5,6.

Joab and Bath-sheba interceded with King David who was unaware of Adonijah's plan, and so Solomon was crowned king; Adonijah the rebel was given another chance and later put to death.

Isn't it strange that the anointed David, the sweet singer, the king after God's own heart, should have his family go to ruin? Even Solomon in old age followed heathen wives into idolatry.

The children of good Christian people do not automatically turn out to be good men or women. There are ways to guarantee that, but David did not follow the Bible rules.

Other godly men in the Bible had sons turn out wrong. Samuel, the blessed prophet of God, made his sons judges in Israel, but we are told: "And his sons walked not in his ways, but turned aside after lucre, and took bribes, and perverted judgment" (I Sam. 8:3). So the people rejected these judges and wanted a king.

It is sadly true today, as in Bible times, that unless earnest, godly people follow particular rules and ways of rearing their children, they are likely to turn out bad, with disgrace to the cause of Christ and broken hearts to those who love them.

II. SOME BLESSED CASES OF WELL-REARED CHILDREN OF BIBLE CHARACTERS

But the children of God's people need not turn out to be wicked, need not be lost. The sweet promise of Proverbs 22:6 is, "Train up a child in the way he should go: and when he is old, he will not depart from it." So we may be sure that where children go wrong, there was a failure on the part of those who reared them.

But there are a number of cases in the Bible where godly people so reared their children that they followed in God's way, and it is a comfort to read about them.

1. Abraham So 'Commanded His Children and His Household After Him' That They Served the Lord

It was no accident that Isaac turned out to be a godly man, for in Genesis 18:17,18 we see God's estimate of the man: "And the Lord said, Shall I hide from Abraham that thing which I do; Seeing that Abraham shall surely become a great and mighty nation, and all the nations of the earth shall be blessed in him?"

So we find that Isaac seemed not to waver when Abraham was ready to offer him as a sacrifice to God on the altar on Mount Moriah! Abraham's influence over Isaac was so great that he could marry only a woman from the group blessed of God, not from among the heathen.

And since God knew that Abraham would "command

his children and his household after him," I am sure that the influence of Abraham on Ishmael was good. Although he was counted as a wild man, he was not a wicked man but was blessed of God. And the details are not given about the lives of any of the later children born to Abraham and Keturah after Sarah's death (Gen. 25:1-6), but we are sure that the godly influence of Abraham did not fail with them.

2. Joshua Made Sure His Whole Household Served the Lord

In Joshua, chapter 24, we read that Joshua called all the tribes of Israel to Shechem—he called for elders, heads and judges and officers. Then he said to them:

"Now therefore fear the Lord, and serve him in sincerity and in truth: and put away the gods which your fathers served on the other side of the flood, and in Egypt; and serve ye the Lord. And if it seem evil unto you to serve the Lord, choose you this day whom ye will serve; whether the gods which your fathers served that were on the other side of the flood, or the gods of the Amorites, in whose land ye dwell: but as for me and my house, we will serve the Lord."—Josh. 24:14,15.

Not only did Joshua and his family serve the Lord; it went to all his household, kin people, and the elders of Israel. In fact, we read in Joshua 24:31, "And Israel served the Lord all the days of Joshua, and all the days of the elders that overlived Joshua, and which had known all the works of the Lord, that he had done for Israel." But that is so important and it is stated emphatically again in Judges 2:7.

The Bible does not give any details of the children of

Joshua. We can only know that they were a part of that whole nation that pledged themselves and did serve the Lord as Joshua lived and as long as those elders who made the pledges overlived Joshua.

3. The Rechabites Wonderfully Followed the Godly Teaching of Their Father Jonadab

In II Kings 10:15 and 23 Jonadab is spelled Jehonadab. And there we find that this man was already well known as a godly man. Jehu took him in his chariot and took him to see the slaying of the priests of Baal.

And this man had an amazing influence over his descendants and kinsmen. This is shown in a wonderfully refreshing story in Jeremiah 35:1-11. Read that story here:

"The word which came unto Jeremiah from the Lord in the days of Jehoiakim the son of Josiah king of Judah, saying, Go unto the house of the Rechabites, and speak unto them, and bring them into the house of the Lord, into one of the chambers, and give them wine to drink.

"Then I took Jaazaniah the son of Jeremiah, the son of Habaziniah, and his brethren, and all his sons, and the whole house of the Rechabites; And I brought them into the house of the Lord, into the chamber of the sons of Hanan, the son of Igdaliah, a man of God, which was by the chamber of the princes, which was above the chamber of Maaseiah the son of Shallum, the keeper of the door: And I set before the sons of the house of the Rechabites pots full of wine, and cups, and I said unto them, Drink ye wine.

"But they said, We will drink no wine: for Jonadab the son of Rechab our father commanded us, saying, Ye shall drink no wine, neither ye, nor your sons for ever: Neither

shall ye build house, nor sow seed, nor plant vineyard, nor have any: but all your days ye shall dwell in tents; that ye may live many days in the land where ye be strangers. Thus have we obeyed the voice of Jonadab the son of Rechab our father in all that he hath charged us, to drink no wine all our days, we, our wives, our sons, nor our daughters; Nor to build houses for us to dwell in: neither have we vineyard, nor field, nor seed: But we have dwelt in tents, and have obeyed, and done according to all that Jonadab our father commanded us.

"But it came to pass, when Nebuchadrezzar king of Babylon came up into the land, that we said, Come, and let us go to Jerusalem for fear of the army of the Chaldeans, and for fear of the army of the Syrians: so we dwell at Jerusalem."

God uses this faithful man and his descendants as an example to the whole house of Israel. He told Jeremiah to tell them, "The words of Jonadab the son of Rechab, that he commanded his sons not to drink wine, are performed; for unto this day they drink none, but obey their father's commandment: notwithstanding I have spoken unto you, rising early and speaking; but ye hearkened not unto me" (Jer. 35:14).

Jonadab had taught his kinsmen and his sons two simple lessons. One, they were never to drink wine: "Ye shall drink no wine, neither ye, nor your sons for ever." The other commandment he had told them has wonderful meaning: they were not to get into the sinful cities but they were to retire away from the mass of people and live in tents and thus separate themselves from the wickedness of this people who were under God's reproach, who would go into captivity. And they obeyed in both matters.

When Nebuchadrezzar's army came into the land, they

were temporarily forced into the city. But they were teaching their children and living to prove they did not belong to this wicked world and they would not be influenced by the idolatry, the drinking, the wickedness of the people about them.

And now here is the remarkable part: the incident when Jehu and Jonadab met in II Kings 10:15 was about 884 B.C., according to Ussher's chronology. But the testing in the days of Jeremiah is timed at about 590 B.C., nearly two hundred years later! And here is a whole sub-tribe, a whole group of godly people, keeping themselves apart from the wickedness around them, and not one of them would drink wine because Jonadab's son Rechab had so taught them. That godly man's influence pervaded a whole group of perhaps hundreds of descendants through about two hundred years.

4. The Prophet Hanani Had a Blessed Son, the Prophet Jehu, Who Followed in His Father's Footsteps Faithfully, Even Through Suffering

King Asa of Judah was a good man, but when he was threatened by Baasha, king of Israel, he brought the silver and gold out of the treasury of the house of the Lord and the king's house and sent them to Ben-hadad, king of Syria, asking him to break his league with Baasha and come to his help, which he did.

That compromise was wrong. And God had a good man to rebuke him. Second Chronicles 16:7-10 says:

"And at that time Hanani the seer came to Asa king of Judah, and said unto him, Because thou hast relied on the king of Syria, and not relied on the Lord thy God, therefore

is the host of the king of Syria escaped out of thine hand. Were not the Ethiopians and the Lubims a huge host, with very many chariots and horsemen? yet, because thou didst rely on the Lord, he delivered them into thine hand. For the eyes of the Lord run to and fro throughout the whole earth, to shew himself strong in the behalf of them whose heart is perfect toward him. Herein thou hast done foolishly: therefore from henceforth thou shalt have wars. Then Asa was wroth with the seer, and put him in a prison house; for he was in a rage with him because of this thing. And Asa oppressed some of the people the same time."

It takes more courage to rebuke a good man than to rebuke a bad man. Preachers more often fail to rebuke the modernism and compromise of Christian leaders than to denounce drunkenness and theft. And it is harder to rebuke a king than to rebuke one's equal.

John the Baptist rebuked King Herod. Paul openly preached the Gospel to Felix, to Festus and Agrippa, and so Hanani rebuked King Asa. Asa was so angry that he put the preacher in jail.

Now here comes the interesting part. Asa had a son, King Jehoshaphat of Judah. Like his father, he compromised. In this case he went with wicked Ahab of the northern kingdom of Israel to the battle of Ramoth-gilead and there Ahab was killed. Now, King Jehoshaphat, following perhaps the philosophy of his father (and both of them good men but wrong in this matter), needed some prophet of God to rebuke him. And God had such a prophet. We read in II Chronicles 19:1-3:

"And Jehoshaphat the king of Judah returned to his house in peace to Jerusalem. And Jehu the son of Hanani the seer went out to meet him, and said to king

Jehoshaphat, Shouldest thou help the ungodly, and love them that hate the Lord? therefore is wrath upon thee from before the Lord. Nevertheless there are good things found in thee, in that thou hast taken away the groves out of the land, and hast prepared thine heart to seek God."

And who was that prophet who came to rebuke Jehoshaphat? It was "Jehu the son of Hanani the seer." As Hanani had rebuked Asa, so his son Jehu, also a prophet of God, rebuked young King Jehoshaphat.

I am sure that Heaven rejoices when a godly preacher has a son who feels he must preach.

Jehu greatly admired his father. He was saved. From his father, he learned to love and trust the true God. He learned that Christians ought not compromise. He learned that a prophet of God ought to rebuke sin even in the king. And he faithfully stood up for God and righteousness just as his father had done before the king.

We do not know any more about Jehu, the son of Hanani, but we know enough. He was a man of God like his father.

5. John the Baptist, a Child of Prayer, Followed His Godly Parents

After perhaps twenty-five or thirty years of earnest prayer, when Zacharias and his wife Elisabeth were both old and well stricken in years, God answered their prayer and gave the son, John the Baptist. The story is told sweetly in Luke 1:1-17. And what kind of a son shall he be? The angel said, "For he shall be great in the sight of the Lord, and shall drink neither wine nor strong drink; and he shall be filled with the Holy Ghost, even from his mother's womb. And many of the children of Israel shall he turn to the Lord their God." One verse tells of the simple rearing of John the Baptist, Luke 1:80, "And the child grew, and waxed strong in spirit, and was in the deserts till the day of his shewing unto Israel."

John was given in answer to prayer and no doubt Elisabeth had begged God for a son who would not be like the drunken priests she knew. She wanted a prophet of God who would turn many people to God. That prayer was heard.

We know that John was reared simply. He was not spoiled. He was loved and kept for the Lord. We know how he turned out, so we know something about his rearing. He followed a godly path from a godly father and mother.

6. Timothy Was Reared on the Bible!

Timothy was the son of a Jewish woman who believed, but his father was a Greek. Paul found him, perhaps, when he was in his teens and took the young man under his wing and he became a great helper and then a pastor.

How the Apostle Paul loved Timothy! He wrote the people at Corinth, "For this cause have I sent unto you Timotheus, who is my beloved son, and faithful in the Lord. . ." (I Cor. 4:17). Again he wrote to them, "Now if Timotheus come, see that he may be with you without fear: for he worketh the work of the Lord, as I also do" (I Cor. 16:10). And to the Christians at Philippi he wrote, "But I trust in the Lord Jesus to send Timotheus shortly unto you, that I also may be of good comfort, when I know your state. For I have no man likeminded, who will naturally care for your state. For all seek their own, not the things which are Jesus Christ's. But ye know the proof of him, that, as a son with the father, he hath served with me in the gospel" (Phil. 2:19-22).

But where did the rearing of Timothy come in? In II Timothy 3:15 Paul says to Timothy, "And that from a child thou hast known the holy scriptures, which are able to make thee wise unto salvation through faith which is in Christ Jesus." He had known the Scriptures from a child! He was taught by a godly mother and grandmother. For in the same epistle, Paul had already written to him, "When I call to remembrance the unfeigned faith that is in thee, which dwelt first in thy grandmother Lois, and thy mother Eunice; and I am persuaded that in thee also" (II Tim. 1:5). Timothy's mother was a Jewish believer; her mother Lois was also a believer. They had taught the boy Timothy from a child the Holy Scriptures and there dwelt in him the "unfeigned faith." Although his father was a Greek and presumably not converted in Timothy's early years, yet that godly mother and grandmother taught Timothy the Word of God, and much of it he memorized and he learned to believe in the God of his mother, and to serve Him.

Thank God, we do not need to let our children grow up as animals, grow up as an untended garden. We can bring them up in the nurture and admonition of the Lord" (Eph. 6:4). We can obey the command, "Train up a child in the way he should go: and when he is old, he will not depart from it" (Prov. 22:6).

III. THE PRINCIPLES THAT ARE A SURE SUCCESS IN REARING CHILDREN FOR GOD

Yes, we said "a sure success." This Scripture says, "Train up a child in the way he should go: and when he is old, he will not depart from it." And there are other promises like that of Psalm 1:1-3, that a Christian avoiding bad company and meditating day and night in the Word of God is guaranteed, ". . .and whatsoever he doeth shall prosper." Let us say that God's plan for a Christian home works, and we should simply set out to follow His rules and trust Him to bring the results that He wants us to have.

Timothy, with a godly mother who taught him the Scriptures and a grandmother who helped in that, turned out to be a wonderful man of God, although his father was a Gentile and, we suppose, unsaved, in Timothy's boyhood.

The Rechabites faithfully served the Lord, keeping the vows impressed upon them by Jonadab their father for some two hundred years! The lad Joseph, away from home, a slave in a foreign country, still stedfastly served the Lord. Whatever the circumstances a Christian is compelled to be in, he can have the blessing of God, and Christian parents can raise godly children.

1. Probably the Greatest Single Requirement in the Home Is Discipline, Authority

The first great commandment about the home is, "Honour thy father and thy mother: that thy days may be long upon the land which the Lord thy God giveth thee" (Exod. 20:12). And Ephesians 6:2 calls this "the first commandment with promise."

But children only honor their parents if the parents exercise their authority and require the honor and obedience due them.

In Ephesians 6:4 is the command, "Ye fathers, provoke

not your children to wrath: but bring them up in the nurture and admonition of the Lord." That word "nurture" really means discipline (see margin). The Greek word there translated nurture is *paideia* and is defined in Young's Analytical Concordance as "nurture, instruction, chastening." That word is translated "chastening" three times in Hebrews 12:5,7 and 11, and the verb form of the word is translated "chasten" six times. Another form of the verb is translated "chastise in Luke 23:16 and 22, where Pilate said about Jesus, "I will therefore chastise him, and release him."

So fathers ought to bring up children in the chastening and admonition of the Lord. And here God puts chastening before instruction. Chastising of a child is the part of love, for Proverbs 13:24 says, "He that spareth his rod hateth his son: but he that loveth him chasteneth him betimes." We are instructed, "Chasten thy son while there is hope, and let not thy soul spare for his crying" (Prov. 19:18). Begin early and when you chastise do it thoroughly and get honest repentance.

We have the promise, "Thou shalt beat him with the rod, and shalt deliver his soul from hell" (Prov. 23:14). Evidently one of the biggest influences in getting children saved is when they are punished for their sins and learn that sin cannot get by and they grow a conscience for sin. Thus they are easier to win to Christ. "Thou shalt beat him with the rod, and shalt deliver his soul from hell."

There are two sweet promises in Proverbs 29:

"The rod and reproof give wisdom: but a child left to himself bringeth his mother to shame."—vs. 15.

"Correct thy son, and he shall give thee rest; yea, he shall give delight unto thy soul."—vs. 17.

So when God says, "Train up a child in the way he should go: and when he is old, he will not depart from it," He has in mind vigorous, corporal punishment for the child when needed. And if it is thorough and one begins early and is consistent, the time for rebellion and needed punishment will soon largely disappear.

The Scripture tells us, "Then Adonijah the son of Haggith exalted himself, saying, I will be king," intending to seize the throne of David. We are also told, "And his father had not displeased him at any time in saying, Why hast thou done so?" (I Kings 1:5,6). The proverb is true: "A child left to himself bringeth his mother to shame."

And the father and mother who lack the character to punish their children will have much unhappiness over the ruin they thus encourage in their children.

We should remember that the thing God commended in Abraham about his family was, "For I know him, that he will *command* his children and his household after him" (Gen. 18:19). Abraham did not simply pray for Isaac to be a good boy nor advise him that he hoped he would do better. He commanded Isaac and Ishmael, and the very term involves discipline.

Note the boldness of Joshua's solemn vow: ". . .as for me and my house, we will serve the Lord" (Josh. 24:15). Joshua was a soldier. He had good discipline in his armies. He was a vigorous character, and he obeyed the Lord by having wicked Achan put to death. We can be sure that when Joshua determined that he and his family would all serve the Lord, he enforced his orders on that matter and they were obeyed.

It is a remarkable fact that even among unsaved people the father and the mother who demand obedience and who punish disobedience and have the honor that God says parents should have in their children, turn out good children and they are easy to win to Christ. That was illustrated in the case of Cornelius in Acts, chapter 10. The man and all his family and kinspeople were saved the same day Peter came and preached to them. He had all the family there and they were all converted. There is good evidence that this man who wanted so badly to do right and have God's blessing, commanded his children and enforced his commands.

And it is also a glad fact that when the Philippian jailer was saved, his whole family was saved. We can well believe that soldiers, law enforcement officers, and others who are accustomed to enforcing discipline, rear their children a little more successfully than many other people do.

I knew a man years ago, a next door neighbor—he was unsaved. I could not win him. But his children were so carefully supervised and the father was so vigorous in his discipline and his supervision that the big family of young people had good convictions. They were moral and clean. They each had a conscience about sin. It was a great joy to me to be able to win those young people to Christ. It was easy because they had grown up under good discipline.

Even the father and mother who pray will not raise their children right unless they do more than pray. Prayer is all right when you obey the Lord about other matters, but prayer will not take the place of obedience in the way of raising children.

The complaint God had about Eli was, "His sons made themselves vile, and he restrained them not" (I Sam. 3:13). Eli did not restrain his sons with chastening when they were younger; now when they were mature, married men, he was high priest and although he had the full authority to have them punished or put them out of the priesthood, he did not. The truth is, the parent who does not punish his children is guilty of a kind of idolatry. So God said to Eli, that he "honourest thy sons above me" (I Sam. 2:29). The right kind of discipline would have saved Eli's family from ruin. It would have saved Absalom and Adonijah from being rebels and Amnon from being a rapist, had David chastened them and ruled them.

2. Diligently Teaching Children to Know, to Love to Obey the Bible, Makes Sure Christian Character

For the Christian who meditates day and night in the Word of God there is a promise, "Whatsoever he doeth shall prosper" (Ps. 1:3). And for the family the command is very plain in Deuteronomy 6:6-9:

"And these words, which I command thee this day, shall be in thine heart: And thou shalt teach them diligently unto thy children, and shalt talk of them when thou sittest in thine house, and when thou walkest by the way, and when thou liest down, and when thou risest up. And thou shalt bind them for a sign upon thine hand, and they shall be as frontlets between thine eyes. And thou shalt write them upon the posts of thy house, and on thy gates."

How vigorous is this requirement! In the home, whenever people sit or stand, when they lie down or rise up, when they walk by the way, they are to be speaking of the Word of God! The Word of God is to be written on the walls of the houses, on the posts of the gates, and people are to carry it in their hands or on their foreheads. What priority God wants the Christian family to give to the Word of God!

There is a saving, redeeming, life-giving power in the Word of God. Any child who learns the promises, the warnings, of the Word of God, who learns to love the Word, to believe it, to live by it, has already pretty well guaranteed maturity of godly character. This surely is a major part in obeying the command, "Train up a child in the way he should go," to make sure that "when he is old, he will not depart from it."

We remember that from a child Timothy had known the Holy Scriptures. They evidently had a great deal to do with making his character.

That means certainly that every home every day ought to have a time of Bible reading and prayer with the whole family. I do not mean simply a verse or two nor a box of "Precious Promises." I mean the whole family should sit and read the Bible together. It is best for all who are able to read to take some part. At my home we found it wise to read in a circle, with each person taking two verses so that all must watch and keep up with the thought. And we had a circle of prayer when everybody prayed every day, and that took priority over school, over getting to work, over doing the dishes.

In the book, *Quest for Souls,* Dr. George W. Truett says:

> Do you have family prayer at your house? Why don't you have it? You might have measured off to you one round thousand years in which to get up your reasons why a Christian parent should not have family prayer in his house, and when the thousand years had passed, you would come back without the semblance of even one reason.
>
> Oh, men and women who love Christ, with your children

growing about you, or already fairly grown, is it possible that human life, invested as it is with such sacred meanings and opportunities and responsibilities, shall go passing away, and the chiefest place of all to get in your witness for Christ, even under your own roof, shall be overlooked and lost! One of the most menacing signs that you can find in any community, if you are able to find it there, is the decay of family prayer in such community.

Again he says:

There was another home of which I would speak. I pleaded with the people one morning in the other years, begging them that they put first things first, and that the men who were Christians would pause at the breakfast table for a little season of prayer with the loved ones around them, or in the evening time, when the day was done, that they would gather the circle about them, and speak with the great King and Saviour in grateful acknowledgment and in continual plea for His mercies to be granted them. Numbers that morning said that they would change their ways.

One outstanding businessman, whose voice was often heard in the city, searched me out and said: "Oh, I have lived miserable far from what is consistent and right. I will turn over a new leaf tonight. Family prayer shall be at my house tonight, and every night henceforth."

I follow it just a moment more. The next morning, as I crossed the city, I saw his only son about fifteen or sixteen years of age, and as I was traveling rapidly along, the son summoned me, and when he reached me, I saw in his face that there was a deep battle of some sort going on, and I said: "What is it, my boy, that I can do for you?" And then he looked down with face averted, and then looked up with his face covered with tears, and said: "You ought to have been at our house last night." "What happened at your house, my boy? I should like to know." He said: "Oh, you should have been there. Papa prayed last night! Papa had sister and me called into the room, and Papa sobbed as he told us he had not lived like a Christian father ought, and Papa asked sister and me to forgive him. Neither of us could talk.We did not know what to say. Both of us cried. Papa asked mother to open the Bible for him, and he tried to read it, but he could not, and then Papa knelt down and prayed, mostly about himself, and then he said when he got up: 'Children, Papa is going to live a different life from this time on.' " And the boy said: "I went to my room and I could not sleep." I said: "Why couldn't you sleep, my boy?" And then, as he leaned over on my shoulder, he said: "I found out last night that I am a sinner, and that I am lost. You do not know how I wanted to see you, that you might tell me what to do."

We turned into a little store house, vacant, and there, in a few words, I told the lad how it is that Jesus saves a sinner, and the lad made his simple, honest surrender, and was saved that very Monday morning. You should have heard him the next Sunday morning, when the pastor said: "Tell us, my boy, what started you in this upward way?" He looked across at his father, on the other side of the house, and said: "Papa's prayer last Sunday night started me in the upward way."

Oh, the home where the whole family reads the Bible and prays together is the home that God will bless and save the children.

3. The Parents Who Honestly Put God and Right Before All Else Can Save Their Children

Lot chose all the rich grasslands around the lower end of the Dead Sea, and moved into wicked Sodom, seeking prosperity without thinking about the awful ruin of his children. Lot's choice of putting business first and choosing the wicked friends who would help that business meant the ruin of his whole family.

And David, for all his love for God, did not reprove his sons for their sins and did not rigorously enforce the discipline which is necessary in every home and doubly necessary sometimes in the home of prominence and wealth.

And we may be sure that David's sin with Bath-sheba and then in having Uriah murdered by the hand of the Ammonites was known to his children. Even if they had not known it, there is something gone from the influence of David because of his sin. And when Nathan told David the parable of the rich man who took a poor man's lamb and killed it (picturing really David's sin in taking Bath-sheba), David had said, "He shall restore fourfold!" But God made that requirement of David. He paid for his sin in the raping of his daughter Tamar. He paid in the murder of Amnon, the guilty son killed by Absalom. He paid in the rebellion of Absalom, which nearly cost him his throne and did cost many lives and much heartbreak. He paid in the death of the baby conceived in David's sin.

Only as a godly father and mother live for God and put God and the Christian life before all else, can the home be assured that the children will follow their godly parents.

We do not mean, of course, just a fundamentalism that is in doctrine and convictions but not in heart's love and joy. Good Christians ought to do right because they delight to do right. We ought to stand up for Christ and the Bible because our heart's love impels us to want to. Children can learn from their parents that it is a joy to be a Christian, a joy to read the Bible, a joy to pray and a joy to win souls.

There is no way to be a good Christian without heart love.

4. The Father and Mother Must Stand Together, Always Agreed on the Great Principles of Rearing the Children

We remember that Isaac and Rebekah were not altogether of one mind about their twin boys, Jacob and Esau. Esau was the favorite of his father; Jacob, the favorite of his mother. It may well be that the mother was more spiritually minded: at least she understood that Jacob was to inherit the headship of the Jewish race and the ancestry of the Lord Jesus. But her scheming may have alienated Esau from the Lord. It did certainly make him an enemy of Jacob and put murder in his heart. It seems she encouraged Jacob in deceit, and together they hoodwinked his old father to get the blessing which God would have seen that he got anyway.

I think that always trouble comes in the home when the parents do not agree about what they require of the children and about insisting on obedience and on punishing sin.

My father used to say, when some of us children (six of us at home) would quarrel, "We do not want any fussing here. When you hear Mamma and me disagreeing and fussing, then you can fuss, too." But they never quarreled. If there was ever any difference of opinion, they settled that difference quietly and alone. If one of them thought a child deserved chastisement, the other agreed. There was never any division of authority.

Sometimes the mother has a favorite child and protects that child from the work or from the discipline that he ought to have. That may be part of the reason for the difference in Cain and Abel. Cain was the firstborn. The mother fondly said, "I have gotten a man from the Lord."

And it may be she thought this firstborn baby in the world was the Messiah. He turned out to be a murderer. For some good reason Abel was a good man, one who was righteous and one who trusted in God. And Cain was a rebel against God and against his brother. That difference may well have been caused because of a mother's favoring Cain.

I know a family where, among four children, the older boy was always given preference. He was Mamma's pride and joy. When he hurt or tormented the other children, she was quick to excuse him so as to protect him from punishment. She had good general principles, but that older boy was always a special case. He is the only one of the family who is not a good Christian. He early sought liberal friends, espoused the doctrines of Karl Marx. He is not a useful Christian. What I saw long ago and foretold has come to pass. A child who is not punished for his sin and not held accountable as he ought to be, is likely to go wrong.

This means that a part of the requirement for a really Christian home is that the wife must be subject to her husband. God intends the man, like Joshua, to take the principal responsibility, and He expects the wife to be subject to her husband and join heartily into his plans and to help enforce his rulings. The husband and the wife must be united for a division here, and thus taking the part of the child who does wrong may lead to great harm.

Two or three years ago there came a letter from a northern state. A family in deep distress wrote about the fifteen-year-old girl in the home. The stepfather had hesitated and perhaps that girl's mother had encouraged that hesitation to take active rule over the children. Now the fifteen-year-old girl was staying out late at night. She rebelled against her mother and defied her. What should they do?

I wrote them that I feared they would not do what I knew they ought to do but that I must tell them anyway. I said to them that, first of all, the husband and the wife together must agree that only a strong course of action could be followed and they must be perfectly agreed upon it. And I said that the next time the girl sassed her mother or was disobedient or came in past the deadline which they set, the stepfather should simply take her down across his lap and with a razor strop or paddle vigorously spank her until she begged for mercy. And the mother should stand by and say, "That's right! And the next time you disobey you are going to get it twice as hard!"

I told them that a girl of fifteen might now leave home instead of surrendering. But if she went on unchecked and uncontrolled she would certainly go to ruin.

I doubted that they would follow my counsel, but they did. And after a while there came another letter. The mother told how she had wept about it, but she knew I was right and that the girl must learn to obey. So she encouraged her husband and the stepfather did exactly what I had counselled. When the girl came in rebellious and defied her mother, he simply took her and whipped her thoroughly. The girl was astonished, but soon she was very penitent. Now they said she was as reverent and obedient and loving as they could desire. They had saved the girl!

Don't wait too late, but by all means let the husband and wife agree on matters of right and wrong and principle, let both agree on what punishment is necessary, and each one back the other.

5. By All Means Get the Children Saved Early. Make Sure!

I have read many times about mothers who prayed long years for a prodigal son to be saved. Well, I am for a mother praying for the boy. But how much better it would be to follow the Bible plan and get your children saved while they are young! Any home that has family altar and regular prayer and Bible reading, any family where the children are taught right and wrong and the plan of salvation, will find that the children may be won to Christ early. By all means, teach the little ones that they are sinners, that they need forgiveness, that God loves them, that Jesus died for them and that if they will put their trust in Him, He will forgive them and save them. And get them to settle the matter clearly and to make it known before the family and get them to claim the Lord in public services and follow Christ in baptism.

Praying will never take the place of witnessing to your children, pressing upon them the matter of their soul's salvation. Mothers and fathers who live right and read the Bible and pray daily with their children and manifest the authority and so get the honor that God intends parents to have, can win their children to Christ. By all means do that and then with the teaching and discipline and example and the happiness of the Christian home, you can be sure the children will turn out right.

Family Tributes to Dad

By Mrs. John R. Rice

With limited time and limited space, how can I do justice to the world's best father? And of course it is expected to be a wholly unbiased opinion!

I suppose the first item on my list is that he is a loving dad. I have often seen fathers who liked their children after they were big enough to walk and talk, but my children's father liked them when they were tiny. I remember how tenderly and efficiently he bathed the first one when she was only a week old and I was too scared to attempt it. He liked to feed the small ones before they had learned to handle a spoon. And the first thing he taught them to say was, "I love Daddy."

Being a loving father, he liked to be with them—he romped with them and played games with them. I have seen them all lined up, he leading the gang as they ran in a circle through the front room, the kitchen, the dining room and the living room and all somersaulting over the big overstuffed chair in the living room. As they grew older he played tennis with them and tried to teach them to play golf and bowl. He taught them dominoes and other table games. They rode horses and bikes and skated. In skating *they* were the teachers and tried to support and help him.

He entertained our small ones on car trips by making his windshield wipers obey him. When he wanted to make them stop he would say to the children, "Now watch." Pointing to the wiper he would say, "Stop," and the wiper would stop. He would do it again and again and they looked with wonder. They never did catch him putting his foot on the accelerator, then lifting it to cause the wiper to start and stop.

He liked to give them thrills in driving. Once he drove a little too far out into the Gulf of Mexico and the waves went over the spark plugs and killed the engine. He had a little trouble getting out that time, but he thought the fun was worth it.

He sang with them for hours on long car trips. Many a roundelay they had—"Old MacDonald had a farm. . ." and

Away down yonder, not so very far off,
A bluejay died of the whooping cough.
He coughed so hard with the whooping cough
That he coughed his head and his tail right off!

He especially liked "The Beatitudes" in a beautiful round they had learned at school. Each Christmas they sang together many, many carols, and as they grew older they began to sing "The Messiah" at Christmastime. They had the help of boyfriends, some of whom later became husbands and stayed on to sing every Christmas large sections of the great oratorio. Strangely enough, the fellows the girls liked all liked music, and since they are married each couple has its own duet. Once a friend asked, "Do all the boys who marry Rice girls have to be singers?" I suppose they would have to like to sing. A singing dad set an example they could not ignore.

In a household where six girls each practiced on a musical instrument—violin, piano, accordion, and clarinet—or practiced vocal exercises, the father never complained about the noise. He might be reading or playing a game in the room next to the music practice room, and with only an open archway between, but he did not mind the screeching of the violin or sour notes made on the instruments.

Along with all the fun went work and responsibility. Our dad insisted that "anyone who did not work was not worth his salt." Their beds were to be made as soon as they were up, and other duties were to be performed religiously. Duty and work were spiritual matters.

Besides the work at home they were expected to join their dad in his effort to get out the Gospel. Before they could operate a typewriter or addressing machine in the office they could help give out circulars about revivals, they could run errands, or clean the office. By the time they were in junior high school they were regularly helping in the office, and in high school they took courses in typing and shorthand getting ready to be better helpers.

Dr. Rice was a good disciplinarian, firm and consistent. He knew how to apply the rod when the rod was needed. Our dad set the standards for our house. He decided when the children should get up and when they should go to bed. He set the hours for them to be home when they went out evenings. They were never confused about what was expected of them and were convinced that Dad's standards were right, no matter what the rest of the world did or thought. The family ate together and thoroughly enjoyed being together. There was never a problem of the children wanting to be out somewhere else for fun—they had more fun at home; a good dad saw to that. They still like one another, still prefer one another's company. There was no generation gap in our family, and there still isn't. Our girls thought their dad was the smartest man in the world and the best man. And they still think so.

They felt perfectly free to go to him with any problem. They knew they would have a sympathetic ear. They talked of anything and everything with their dad. Their boyfriends came under his scrutiny, and the girls listened when he gave them advice. If he said, 'That one has very poor manners—he is very impolite,' or made other observations, they took them to heart.

They had great delight in the times of family devotions, when we sat at the table after breakfast and read the Bible and prayed. We read the Bible completely through, again and again. Our girls now say that they learned the important lessons of life during this time. It was during the Bible reading they received their sex education, their lessons in good manners, their social graces, their standards for living, and their comfort for the pressures of the very busy and demanding life in an evangelist's home. They knew they would be watched and that their daddy would be judged by their actions. They were concerned that their daddy's reputation and his straight preaching would not be jeopardized by the way they lived.

Though Dr. Rice has been away from home more than half the time on missions for the Lord, he never left the matter of his children's discipline in the hands of others.

He set the rules when he left. He checked up when he got back. If things had begun to slide a bit in his absence he took things in hand and set them on the right road again. He was determined that in the home of one evangelist he would see that the children turned out right; he was determined under God to turn them out right.

Thank God for a faithful father who took time for his children. He always had time to answer their questions, to know their problems, to teach them the things they needed to know, to pray with them and comfort and guide them as they had need.

I could wish for every child a father like my children's father. While he was winning other children to the Lord, he did not neglect to win his children and train them for the Lord.

"Like As a Father. . ."

By Grace Rice MacMullen

"Like as a father pitieth his children, so the Lord pitieth them that fear him." — Psalm 103:13.

Held in your huge hand, I early, dimly sensed
Security, protection, learned trusting peace.

Hungry, thirsty, needing clothing clean and blanket warm,
The baby I was, somehow found provided.

Grew larger yet, and still in need of these,
Became aware of *you*, providing daily—sustenance, shelter.

And new, still deeper needs were felt—
The longing for understanding; the need for love—for
love implied,
love expressed,
love foundationing each day's actions.

Came laughter, and the joy of playing together;
Skinned knees healed with kisses; sore toes and broken heart alike your tender ministrations knew.

And discipline: Knew you set your heart to guide,
And train and lead, to help—
(and not to help, when *that* was helping most;
though father-heart might yearn to do, to fix, to change.)

The hours you spent mind-stretching: explaining, teaching "whys,"
Set standards; showed the way of best things;
Decried all the ordinary; raised the banner high,
Required the best for God:
To start the task with courage,
To stand strong, alone, if need be, for the right,
To fail, perhaps, take comfort, try again.

You prayed. In trust and earnest faith
You asked, prevailed, received.
I saw God's eagerness to give, His wide resources, endless power—
And knew, as yours had, *His* could all be mine.

I saw you suffer—reproached, rebuked, reviled;
Saw your good evil spoken of.
Saw you remain steadfast, brave, determined,
Saw quiet victory, saw God honored in pain;
Prayed I might meet it thus.

And so I saw God live in you—in person, saw Him walk.
"In the hollow of His hand"—how easy you made
it to be sure God loved and cared for me!

"And my God shall supply all your needs," you said;
I was sure He would; for hadn't you these years
lovingly shown me what a Father is?

"Robes of righteousness" and "garments of praise"
Were what you really were. Could we do less than
pray,
"Let the beauty of the Lord our God be on us"!

Food,—ah yes, I never lacked; but how sweet to
have the appetite aroused
For what you hungered for: the bread of life,
the manna,
the oil of the Spirit,
to fill my life!

And were my prayer to one petition bound, it could be this:
"Oh, make me like my Father—and my dad!"

April, 1970
(Copyrighted)

By Daughter, Mary Lloys Himes

I've been looking back through the years and thinking about what my father, Dr. John R. Rice, has meant to me, as a little child, as a teen-ager, and now as a grown woman.

As a tiny girl, I remember Daddy peeling an orange or an apple for me, cutting my meat at the table. Daddy was the surgeon who with the point of his handy pocketknife removed the little splinters from my finger and comforted me with a kiss. Daddy was the fiery preacher whose sermon on the Second Coming of the Lord was so moving that his five-year-old little daughter, me, couldn't sleep in her bed until she had finally trusted the Lord Jesus as Saviour.

Flying kites, or shooting fireworks or rowing a boat were all great adventures with Daddy. And the night after night of attending revival meetings were a joy. No one ever thought of asking if they had to go!

Later on, softball, tennis and volleyball were great fun with Daddy. He insisted that we help with housework, learn to cook and sew and clean, but we also must work in the office, running machinery, rolling THE SWORD OF THE LORD copies for mailing, learning the most efficient way to do a job. During those adolescent years I remember Daddy singing with us often, challenging us to memorize chapters of the Bible, always learning with us and encouraging us. Daddy coached our girls' trio, encouraged us to practice piano and singing, and paid for innumerable lessons.

When he was away from home in revival meetings, his frequent letters and phone calls reminded us that Daddy loved us. His leading of family devotions taught us to love the Bible, and we each heard him pray for our individual needs.

Daddy was the first to make me aware of my responsibility to win souls. He has constantly been inspiration and example through the years. I still read everything he writes over and over. When I have a special need I want my father to know so he can pray for me.

And to my husband, our five children and me, the joy of being with, and spending leisure time with Daddy and Mother has never abated!

By Daughter, Elizabeth Handford

I'm not sure I can tell you, Daddy, how much you mean to me. It isn't easy to express something I feel so deeply, especially when so many folks will listen in. Besides, how can I crowd a whole lifetime of delight and comfort and learning and caring which you and Mother gave us—how can I crowd all that onto one inadequate blob of paper?

The other day a young wife came for counseling, terribly depressed. I told her God could meet her needs; He could answer her prayers. She looked at me with eyes brimming with tears, "Libby, that's what Mother and Daddy told me for years, but it didn't work for them!" How blessed I felt, when I could answer, "That's what Mother and Daddy told me for years, and thank God, it did work for them!"

Of all the wonderful things you and Mother gave us, this is probably the greatest: the truths you taught us from the Word of God worked for you.

You taught us that God answers prayer. Then you prayed for things—specific, enumerated, definite things. We saw God give you specific answers to your prayers.

You told us what God expected of His children in sacrificial living. Then you demonstrated it. You gave, joyfully and without complaint, of all your resources—money, emotions, time. Remember the poor bums you'd bring home from a mission service, and how, occasionally, they'd be gone before daylight, with what little money there was in the house? "No matter," you'd say, "I'd rather make a mistake helping someone who isn't sincere, than to not help someone who does mean business for the Lord."

How many young preacher boys you fed! How many thousands of dollars you put into printing the books and THE SWORD OF THE LORD, economizing on your personal needs, stretching the meager balance to cover music lessons, and textbooks, and yards of cotton for little girls' dresses. And Mother, bless her dear heart, cheerfully cooperating—enduring all the office equipment for addressing and mailing THE SWORD set up in the dining room, so she couldn't serve supper on Fridays until the mail bags were at the post office. And Mother, who loves pretty things, putting up with the front room as a bookstore, and the back room a Sword office, and the attic storage for all the Sword books. You made THE SWORD a family enterprise, and the methods I learned in those days I've used a thousand times since.

Remember how we threw the packages of *Bible Facts About Heaven* from the printer's truck, bucket-brigade style, up to the third-floor attic? That's once you were grateful for the girls' boyfriends!

You taught us that, since we didn't know how we would be serving the Lord when we grew up, we should learn everything we could about everything. Then, when we saw a job that needed to be done, we'd be ready to do it. You gave us a liberal education—the kind you can't get at school. Think of all those trips! New York, by way of Arkansas, with its bald-knee cyprus in the swamps; Virginia, and Mount Vernon. Liberty Hall in Philadelphia; The Statue of Liberty in the New York harbor, viewed from a small ferry; Niagara Falls; Chicago, and Moody Church. When we're on a trip with our kids, and they complain about being crowded, I say, "Kids, you don't know how lucky you are. Why, when I was a kid, eight of us went to New York in a 1936 Nash, and—" they've heard the story so often they chime in on my punch line!

Thank you for those trips—not just for the sense of history and love of country we soaked up, not just for the basic competence we learned in meeting new situations; but also for the feeling that there was a whole world of wonder and delight, a curiosity about ideas, and things, and functions, that enrich everyday living.

You taught us that God had a perfect will for us, that we could know what He wanted us to do, and that the only thing left to do was to follow His will. I often did not understand all that was involved, but I was always sure that when Daddy said, "This is what God wants us to do," it really was God's will. How I long to give my children the same certainty: you can know God's will; you can do that will.

You taught us there were no double standards. What was right for the children was right for the grownups. Remember when Mother went to Texas and left me in charge of the cooking? I spent the week's grocery money on a bargain case of canned peas—10c a can! You valiantly ate peas for entree, vegetable, salad and dessert, without complaint. And it wasn't until last summer I discovered you don't really care for peas! (Suppose that's why?) You were as demanding on yourself in the large things as in the small, and I thank you with all my heart for this.

You taught us to put the Lord first, even if it meant going to revival meetings every night, weeks on end, and groggily studying in the early morning hours. How else could we have learned so much Scripture, and heard so many great preachers? How else could we have learned a compassion and burden for unsaved people? How else could we have stored the precious memories of being "family" in the car, going to and from the services?

I remember being awakened from a sound slumber to the words, "Jimmy, would you like a tutti-fruitti ice cream cone?" *Tutti fruitti?* Even today the words are mystic and tantalizing. I can't remember the flavor, but I can remember wondering how Daddy knew I'd love a tutti-fruitti cone!

You taught us that families were for loving and for caring. You gave us more personal attention, even when you were away in revivals much of the time, than my friends got from their fathers. You kept track of our studies, our boyfriends, our new enthusiasms, and your letters answered our mixed-up adolescent needs with a tenderness that spilled over the strictness of your decisions, and made them bearable.

Were the rules hard? Yes. Did it hurt to be different? Yes. Did I always understand your decisions? No. But I never doubted that you really cared how I felt—your tears proved that—or that you knew what was the right thing to do.

You taught us that life had many "oughts," but that there was time for fun and joy, too. Remember when you drove down a steep embankment so we could picnic by the river, and then couldn't get the car back up the grade? You drove down the creek bed, to our fearful delight, until you found an easier grade. Remember the tennis games down at Northside Park? Remember jumping to meet the huge waves in the Gulf of Mexico? Remember the hours we spent listening to phonograph records of Caruso and Galli-Curci and "The Stars and Stripes Forever"?

My very earliest memories of you, in the Fort Worth days, are of watching you play with the children—blowing up a long balloon; your trying out Grace's new roller skates and landing in an undignified sprawl at the bottom of the hill; playing a game of "London Bridge" by the fragrant honeysuckle at the back door.

There's another memory from those days. I remember hearing you preach over the radio, and being so convicted of my sins that I couldn't wait for you to get home so I could get saved. (Grace wasn't sure I really got saved, because I smiled so much. She just didn't know how deep the conviction had been, and how sweet was the relief!) You couldn't have given me a greater gift—the assurance of salvation based on the Word of God, and the means for steady spiritual growth.

You taught us so many things, consciously,

systematically, as if you had an itemized list of Things Every Child Has a Right to Know. But you taught us even more when you were not consciously teaching. I watched, and learned, when you spoke gently and reasonably to an angry employee; I watched when you slept but clasped your Bible tight; I heard you praying far into the dark hours of the night; I saw you weep when you took a stand for the fundamentals of the faith, and so lost a lifelong friend. I watched, and learned, and even today measure many an action by "What would my daddy do about this?"

There is more, so much more, I could write. But I thank the Heavenly Father for the gift of a father and mother who loved me enough to discipline me; who, at the sacrifice of personal needs and interests, trained me so that life is filled with joyful, profitable service.

By Jessie Rice Sandberg
(Dr. Rice's daughter No. 4)

Trying to describe my appreciation for a whole lifetime of your love and influence, Dad, is like trying to illustrate Niagara Falls with a glass of water and a washboard. Still, I'd like to offer my "few drops of water" and hope that you can imagine the whole waterfall of appreciation which I feel but cannot express.

Perhaps it will seem strange that the first thing which comes to my mind and therefore the first thing I want to thank you for is *memories*—memories of the special pair of stilts you built for me on my seventh birthday, memories of the times you prayed for me in my childish fears, memories of the sweet, solemn kiss you gave me on my wedding day, memories of the special poems you wrote for me on my birthday and on Valentine's Day, memories of your eager participation in family games and song fests.

The second thing I want to thank you for is your determination to give me as much equipment as possible for a rich and full life. Thank you for insisting on the piano lessons and the voice lessons which I sometimes failed to appreciate but have used since almost every day of my life. Thank you for encouraging me to write and draw and sew. Thank you for teaching me to swim and play softball. Thank you for your patience in showing me how to serve a tennis ball, how to drive a car, and how to find the square root of a number.

The third and most important thing I want to thank you for is your part in developing in me a deep faith in the Lord Jesus Christ. Thank you for your emphasis on early salvation, for your insistance on the importance of Christian fellowship and the habit of faithful attendance at church. Thank you for the constant exposure to the Bible in family devotions and in the everyday events of life. Thank you for teaching by precept and example that God really does answer prayer. Thank you for proving that "he that winneth souls is wise."

Last of all, thank you for your confidence in me, for your constant reminder that I could be anything and do anything God wanted me to be and do. Thank you for providing for me the best example of Christian womanhood a girl could want by marrying the girl who became my mother! Thank you for your constant love and concern and prayers for me in the years since I have left the home nest.

God bless you, dearest Daddy!

By Mrs. Joanna Rice Rice, Daughter Number Five

People have often asked me, "How does it feel to be the daughter of a famous man like Dr. John R. Rice?" I might answer by saying, "Like it feels to know you're loved, of great value to the Lord, and responsible for helping others come to know and love the Lord."

The other day I was telling my husband about how lonely Daddy often was while away from home on speaking engagements. One such time he called long distance and made arrangements for me to be excused from school for a week, take a long train trip alone in order to spend some time with him in a meeting. It was a tremendous week for a thirteen-year-old girl—hearing my dad preach several times every day, eating every meal together, taking walks along the Ohio River bank at night, sharing hot tamales (when mine fell through a grating in the sidewalk he said, "Here, finish mine; I was just eating it to keep you company"), and sharing our hopes and dreams. I thought I was helping my dad and didn't realize until my husband suggested it, twenty-five years later, that Daddy planned it, not because he needed me but because he felt *I* needed some special time with him!

Of course the greatest thing any dad can do for his child is to lead him or her to trust Christ as Saviour, and this my dad did for me. He used my six-year-old selfishness in not sharing the swing to show me my black heart and need of a Saviour and then the next step was easy. How glad I am I settled it then!

It is wonderful to have a dad who cares about each child personally! Some of the outstanding memories I have are these:

Being carried in Daddy's arms at the Texas State Centennial when I was too tired to walk any further. . . .

Being given the title "Daddy's Baby" when a new baby replaced me at age six. . . .

Piling into the car for a trip to the lagoon, hoping the sign would say "Skating Today" when ice skating must have been the last thing a dad would choose after growing up with no skating experience. . . .

Daddy's insisting on my taking piano and voice lessons *and practicing* when there were already four others to pay for and listen to. . . .

Playing all kinds of games with Dad—tennis, golf, croquet, Monopoly, Carroms, volleyball—and usually having him beat us at them all. . . .

Walking around the block one night, telling Daddy all the problems of a high school girl's heart. . . .

Taking him with me to pick out a sport coat for my fiance's Christmas gift. . . .

All this and so much more!

It's wonderful to have a dad who loved me enough to make me mind and spanked me when I didn't, taught me to read and love and memorize the Word of God, taught me by precept and example to pray and expect answers, taught me to respect authority, taught me the joy of sharing, that work is a blessing, and that you can do anything you ought to do.

By Joy Rice Martin
Dr. Rice's baby daughter

As a child, I firmly believed that my dad was the smartest, most loving, and the best preacher of any father in the world. Now, as a mother of five, looking back, I find my opinion has even grown stronger over the years. Dr. John R. Rice, my dad, continues to exemplify the best of earthly fathers. (Thank God that my children have the same kind of wonderful daddy!)

Thinking back over the years, I remember so many

incidents which illustrate my dad's special ways as a father.

As a very tiny girl, I remember kneeling down beside the bed with Daddy for prayer before going to sleep. He was often gone, so those few moments with him in prayer were special.

A little later I remember a very special Sunday afternoon in Hoopeston, Illinois, when as a four-year old I napped with Daddy. I had thought long about the revival messages I had heard from his lips. . . .I had sat on the front row in many of his meetings. So it was natural that on this day I should ask him if I could be saved. We prayed together and I received the Lord Jesus. Soon after that, going home from a revival when he had preached on "Hell" with a great burden, I patted his cheek as he drove and whispered, "Daddy, I'm sure glad I know I'm going to Heaven, aren't you?"

In the following years, Daddy was away from home often, for this was the period of his citywide revival campaigns; Mother was often with him. Going through boxes of mementos from this period, I found dozens of letters from Daddy, all filled with tender expressions of concern, practical wisdom, and sometimes stern warnings for his "baby" daughter. . .but always filled with love and prayer: "Joy, be sure to get up the first time you are called. Are you making your bed?. . .You must be careful to feed Flicka (our dog) and give her plenty of water. . .Don't forget to pray for me." Later admonitions included, "I'm glad you are making good grades. . .Be sure to keep up with your voice practice." And the day came, too, when he commented, "Don't get too serious about dating yet. Remember you have much time ahead of you—don't rush." And always, even after I was in college, the letters closed, "Love, Daddy," with the distinctive O's and X's which denoted hugs and kisses. All six of us girls knew beyond a shadow of doubt that our dad loved us.

All bright memories. . .? No, I remember some tears, too—tears of pain and repentance after a hard spanking. We learned early that disobedience is wrong, and how we hated to displease our dad! To those spankings I attribute my sensitivity toward sin. Thank God for a dad who did right and disciplined even when he grieved over the pain caused!

I have memories of moments of delight and laughter and song—batting a tennis ball with him, watching him on roller skates for the first time when he was over fifty, riding a Ferris wheel with him, singing duets in the car on long trips, riding horses with him.

In our home, meal times with Daddy were a special delight—never a dull moment, or an eager pushing away from the table to escape to more desirable companions. Daddy seemed to know about everything and took an interest in all of our questions.

Daddy and Mother together made home a spiritual center, a school specializing in character training and great Christian truth; we learned by precept and example the values of loyalty, convictions and high standards, and hard work. Many are the sermons on prayer and Bible study I absorbed as a small girl. Frequently the last thing I saw Dad do at night and the first thing in the morning was to read the Bible. Often at night in the room next to mine I would hear him say, "Lord, Jesus, help me." He prayed aloud even in his sleep.

After graduating from college, I worked with him full-time before graduate work and marriage. I saw steadfastness of faith despite jeering letters from enemies and cruelties of friends; I saw patience in tribulation—and sometimes impatience at the foolishness of wayward Christians; I saw hours spent in study of God's Word; I heard prayers in behalf of hundreds of Christians.

These are just a few of the memories I treasure from years with my dad, one whose character and diligence continue to inspire me, and whose love and prayers bring me daily joy.

Thank you, dearest Daddy!

The daughters together. From left to right—Mrs. Joy Martin, Mrs. Joanna Rice, Mrs. Jessie Sandberg, Mrs. Elizabeth Handford, Mrs. Mary Lloys Himes, and Mrs. Grace MacMullen. The poem below was written by them in honor of Dr. Rice's 75th birthday.

GOD BLESS YOU, DAD, ON YOUR 75th BIRTHDAY!

The six of us had tried and tried
To find the gift to please our Dad;
Something common would not do
To show our love in some way new.

But—impossible task! Soon we found
There was no gift suitably grand
To show our thanks for a father's tears,
Love, compassion, through these years.

How does one measure and then repay
Qualities intangible and yet so essential?
Integrity, conviction, purity, zeal,
Firmness combined with sweet appeal!

Foolish thought! to hope any gift,
However fine, could somehow reward
These treasures of soul, heart and mind.
Yes, impossible task, a gift to find.

O God, You know we love him so,
We're not content this day to pass
Without at least some symbol of this grace,
Some token as we these years retrace.

Lord, we know what would please him best
And we'll give it, God help us, forever—
Our lives for Christ, in every way,
Just as Dad showed us day by day.

As wives and mothers, teachers, too,
We'll demonstrate these lessons taught by you
To be prayerful, loving, eager for souls,
Watchful, earnest—these are our goals.

This, dear Dad, is our gift to you,
As we thank God for these good years—
Our promise, our pledge, by God's help to be
The kind of women you've dreamed we would be.

And, watching our walk, our dress, and our talk,
People will say (as they always do),
"Those are the daughters of John R. Rice."
May they also say, "They are daughters of Christ."

—J.R.M.